Exercises in Contemporary English

This workbook is designed to accompany
A Concise Grammar of Contemporary English
by Randolph Quirk and Sidney Greenbaum,
which is based on *A Grammar of Contemporary English*
by Randolph Quirk, Sidney Greenbaum, Geoffrey Leech,
and Jan Svartvik, published by Seminar Press,
a division of Harcourt Brace Jovanovich, Inc.

Exercises
in Contemporary
English

JOHN ALGEO
UNIVERSITY OF GEORGIA

Harcourt Brace Jovanovich, Inc.
NEW YORK   CHICAGO   SAN FRANCISCO   ATLANTA

ISBN: 0-15-512931-7

Library of Congress Catalog Card Number: 74-292

Printed in the United States of America

Preface

These exercises have been designed to accompany A Concise Grammar of Contemporary English (CGCE) by Randolph Quirk and Sidney Greenbaum, with each exercise keyed to a section of that book. For the convenience of students, definitions of many basic terms have been included in the directions preceding each exercise. Although instructors may prefer to supply their own grammatical explanations or to refer their students to other grammars, these exercises closely match the corresponding sections of CGCE.

The exercises fall into several groups. Some are designed to provide students with practice in using the grammatical categories and terms of CGCE by applying them in the analysis of sentences. Some are intended to increase the students' awareness of the structure of English and its grammatical flexibility. Others call the students' attention to usage problems and can serve as the basis for class discussion of the question of correctness. (No attempt has been made to take sides on this question; actually, some of these usage exercises include problematical constructions for which there is no one obviously correct form.) Still others provide the basis for a discussion of nuances between alternate grammatical forms. Throughout the exercises, "grammar-book English" has been avoided in favor of natural, often colloquial, sentences. All the exercises can be answered with the aid of the relevant sections of CGCE; for some a desk dictionary, such as Webster's New Collegiate Dictionary, eighth edition (WNCD), will be useful. A separate Answer Key is available for certain exercises.

With CGCE, this workbook is intended for use in grammar courses that aim to provide knowledge of, and increased competence in, English grammar according to the tradition represented by the reference grammars of Jespersen, Kruisinga, Poutsma, and Quirk, Greenbaum, Leech, and Svartvik. Though CGCE takes into account recent work in the transformational and systemic schools (as well as American structuralism and some other approaches like stratificationalism), it makes use of what those schools have pointed out about English grammar with minimal emphasis on their theoretical procedures: it is concerned with the facts of English more than with theories about those facts. Thus, while these exercises are compatible with transformational or other approaches to grammar, they view English primarily from the standpoint of an enlightened traditionalism.

I gratefully acknowledge the help of Dwight L. Bolinger (Harvard University), O. C. Dean (University of Georgia), Sidney Greenbaum

(University of Wisconsin, Milwaukee), and Randolph Quirk (University of London), each of whom read part or all of the exercises and offered valuable suggestions for their improvement. I am also pleased to acknowledge Natalie Bowen's perceptive editorial help and April Maddox's skillful assistance in the preparation of the manuscript. And especially I am grateful to Adele Algeo, who helped at every stage in every way.

JOHN ALGEO

Contents

● Adjectives and Adverbs   69–85

● Prepositions and Prepositional Phrases   86–92

● **The Complex Noun Phrase**   183–196

● **Focus, Theme, and Emphasis**   197–207

Appendix I. Word Formation   208–213

Exercises in Contemporary English

NAME _____ SCORE _____

● 1.1 Regional Variation: Words and Sounds (Ref: CGCE 1.1–3)

DIRECTIONS The way Americans use English varies from place to place: we all speak some regional dialect or some mixture of dialects. Answer the questions by circling the response or responses that seem most normal to you. If you think of an answer you prefer that is not listed, add it. Ignore the numbers in parentheses for the moment.

1. What do you call a container for water used in mopping and the like?
   bucket (3, 4), pail (2)

2. What do you call a fixture for drawing water in a sink?
   faucet (2), hydrant, spicket, spigot, tap (3, 4)

3. What do you call a utensil for frying food?
   fry pan (1), frying pan (1), skillet (3, 4), spider (2)

4. What do you call a small stream?
   branch (3b, 4), brook (2), creek (1), kill (2), run (3a)

5. What do you call an animal with a white stripe and a bad odor?
   polecat (3, 4), skunk (2, 3), woodpussy (3)

6. What do you call a soft, lumpy, white kind of cheese?
   (bonny) clabber cheese (3, 4), cottage cheese (1), curds, curd cheese (3, 4), Dutch cheese (2), pot cheese (2), smearcase (3a), sourmilk cheese (1)

7. What do you call an insect with large wings, common around water?
   (devil's) darning needle (2), dragonfly (1), mosquito hawk (4), snake feeder (3, 4), snake doctor (3b, 4)

8. What do you call a strip of concrete or the like, next to a street, for use by pedestrians?
   pavement (3), sidewalk, walk (1)

9. How is *greasy* pronounced?
   greassy (2), greazy (3, 4)

10. Which word does *creek* rime with?
    peek (1), pick (2, 3a)

11. Which word has the same final sound as *with*?
    boot (2), smooth (2), tooth (1)

12. Which pairs of words, if any, are pronounced alike?
    lager/logger (2), cot/caught (3a), barn/born (3b), born/borne (3a), pin/pen (4)

1

1.2   Regional Variation: Grammar and Areas   (Ref: CGCE 1.1–3)

DIRECTIONS   Answer the questions by circling the response or responses that seem most likely to you. If you prefer an answer not listed, add it.

1. About diving, you might say, "Yesterday, I _____ into the pool once."
   dived (1), dove (2)

2. About biting, you might say, "The dog has _____ the mailman."
   bit (3), bitten (1)

3. If you are nauseated, you might say, "I'm sick _____ my stomach."
   at (3, 4), in (3), on (3a), to (2)

4. If the time is 9:50, you might say, "It is ten _____ ten."
   before (1), of (2), till (3, 4), to (4)

5. To several persons, you might say, "I've got something for _____."
   you (1), you-all or y'all (3b, 4), you-uns (3), youse or yuz (2)

6. If you want to alight from a bus, you might say, " I want _____."
   off (3), to get off (1)

7. If you are expecting a friend, you might say, "I'm waiting _____ him."
   for (1), on (3)

DIRECTIONS   The numbers after the responses above and in the preceding exercise (1.1) represent the areas in which those responses are most likely to be found: 1) throughout the U.S.; 2) North; 3) Midland; 3a) northern Midland; 3b) southern Midland; 4) South. What area do most of your responses belong to? On the map below, locate the area or areas where you grew up and where you now live or have lived. Locate also the areas where your parents grew up and lived.

1.3 American and British Words and Grammar (Ref: CGCE 1.4–9; WNCD)

DIRECTIONS Match the terms with approximately the same meanings.

	BRITISH	AMERICAN		BRITISH	AMERICAN
1. _____	bonnet	a. dessert	13. _____	chemist	a. billboard
2. _____	boot	b. fruit course	14. _____	billion	b. baby carriage
3. _____	caravan	c. garter	15. _____	draughts	c. checkers
4. _____	crisp	d. hood	16. _____	elevenses	d. coffee break
5. _____	dessert	e. potato chip	17. _____	football	e. 14 pounds
6. _____	lorry	f. sneakers	18. _____	hoarding	f. druggist
7. _____	plimsolls	g. subway	19. _____	petrol	g. gas
8. _____	suspender	h. trailer	20. _____	pram	h. nurse
9. _____	sweet	i. truck	21. _____	treacle	i. molasses
10. _____	tube	j. trunk	22. _____	underground	j. subway
11. _____	vest	k. undershirt	23. _____	sister	k. soccer
12. _____	waistcoat	l. vest	24. _____	stone	l. trillion

DIRECTIONS Each sentence contains an expression that is characteristically British. Rephrase the sentence, substituting a characteristically American expression.

25. [—Do you think they opened the doors?] —They may have done.

_____

26. My hypochondriacal aunt really *is* in hospital now.

_____

27. He has a bookshop in the High Street.

_____

28. I've just got a good idéa.

_____

29. Australia are playing Canada next week; both teams are good.

_____

30. Have they any chance?

_____

1.4   American and British Sounds and Spellings

(Ref: CGCE 1.4–9; WNCD)

DIRECTIONS   Indicate which pronunciation is typically American (A) and which is typically British (B) by writing the appropriate letter in the blank.

1. *a'luminum* _____; *,alu'minium* _____

2. *ancillary*, stressed *an'cillary* _____; or *'ancil,lary* _____

3. *ate*, riming with *wet* _____; or with *wait* _____

4. *clerk*, riming with *work* _____; or with *lark* _____

5. *comrade*, ending like *raid* _____; or like *rad* _____

6. *corollary*, stressed *'corol,lary* _____; or *co'rollary* _____

7. *laboratory*, stressed *la'boratory* _____; or *'labora,tory* _____

8. *lieutenant*, beginning like *loo* _____; or like *leff* _____

9. *medicine*, pronounced in three syllables _____; or *med'cine* _____

10. *missile*, pronounced *missīle* _____; or *miss'le* _____

11. *patriot*, beginning like *pat* _____; or like *pay* _____

12. *privacy*, pronounced *prī-vacy* _____; or *prĭv-acy* _____

13. *schedule*, beginning like *sh* _____; or like *sk* _____

14. *solder*, beginning like *sod* _____; or like *sold* _____

15. *vitamin*, beginning like *vite* _____; or like *vitt* _____

DIRECTIONS   Indicate which spelling is typically American (A) and which is typically British (B).

16. centre _____; center _____

17. check _____; cheque _____

18. color _____; colour _____

19. connexion _____; connection _____

20. kerb _____; curb _____

21. draft _____; draught _____

22. pajamas _____; pyjamas _____

23. tire _____; tyre _____

24. waggon _____; wagon _____

4

1.5 Standard and Nonstandard English (1) (Ref: CGCE 1.2–9)

DIRECTIONS The following sentences illustrate uses that are nonstandard for any of several reasons: they may be educationally substandard, or regionally limited, or otherwise restricted in their contexts. Circle the nonstandard part of the sentence and rewrite that part in the blank.

EXAMPLE I don't want (no) cake.   **any**

1. There is a lot of people outside the store. _____
2. They play their stereo softer anymore. _____
3. She couldn't find a copy of *War and Peace* anywheres. _____
4. The squirrels were a-chattering in the trees. _____
5. I have a banana in one hand and a orange in the other. _____
6. For a time, things looked badly, but they are better now. _____
7. He's going to summer school on account of he needs credits. _____
8. Somebody rung the doorbell. _____
9. They put dynamite in the old hotel and blowed it up. _____
10. The bubble finally bursted. _____
11. It don't matter at all. _____
12. I've never drank coffee as hot as this. _____
13. He almost drownded in the lake. _____
14. I want for him to enjoy himself. _____
15. She did the job good. _____
16. She advised me as regards to my courses. _____
17. Please leave him go. _____
18. I like to fell off the chair laughing. _____
19. They could of told us where to look. _____
20. We're nowheres near finished yet. _____

5

1.6   Standard and Nonstandard English (2)   (Ref: CGCE 1.2–9)

DIRECTIONS   The following sentences illustrate uses that are nonstandard for any of several reasons: they may be educationally substandard, or regionally limited, or otherwise restricted in their contexts. Circle the nonstandard part of the sentence and rewrite that part in the blank.

EXAMPLE   I don't want (no) cake.   <u>**any**</u>

1. He stood on line an hour to get tickets. _____
2. I seen him at the Union this morning. _____
3. Either he put on weight or his clothes shrinked. _____
4. There is no such a word as *quarm*. _____
5. I'll learn you not to be late. _____
6. These here books are not mine. _____
7. She found them books you wanted. _____
8. I hoped you was finished. _____
9. Don't open the door without I tell you. _____
10. I've wrote the paper already. _____
11. If youse want it, there's plenty of dessert. _____
12. They missed the bus theirselves. _____
13. We might could help if you want us to. _____
14. Let's us not get excited now. _____
15. Nobody told us where to look neither. _____
16. You didn't need to remind us because we'd have gone anyways. _____
17. I wish you had of told me that before. _____
18. We can't skate any more, but we used to could. _____
19. He wants that we should help him. _____
20. Did they suspicion anything from what you said? _____

1.7   Stylistic Variety   (Ref: CGCE 1.10–15)

DIRECTIONS   The following sentences illustrate uses that vary in standard English according to a style. Circle the form you would use in normal conversation with a friend. Be prepared to discuss the circumstances under which the other forms might be used.

1. I'm lucky to have found my watch, (ain't I / am I not / aren't I)?
2. Gerald will meet us for lunch (about / at about / at approximately) 12:30.
3. Everybody has (his / his or her / their) work done.
4. William (didn't use to / never used to / usedn't to) be such a good archer.
5. I (dreamed / dreamt) I was an astronaut on my way to Mars.
6. He'll do it when he is (good and / quite) ready.
7. Since it was fixed, the phonograph works (good / well).
8. Marie (had better / should) finish quickly.
9. We (can / can't) hardly see in this fog.
10. Tony has a vegetable garden (back of / behind / in back of) his house.
11. It's (I / me) they are looking for.
12. The weather looks (kind of / rather) uncertain today.
13. They had (lots of / many) chances to learn bridge.
14. The reason he is moving is (because / that) he has a new job.
15. I (will / shall) make an appointment for Saturday.
16. If you drive (slow / slowly), you'll save gas.
17. (Who / Whom) did you meet downtown?
18. We have a long (way / ways) to go before dark.
19. Sam likes (these / this) kind of books.
20. She is doing it (as / like / the way) she was told.

1.8   Divided Usage

DIRECTIONS   The following sentences illustrate uses that vary in standard English. Both options are widely used in a variety of contexts, but some speakers prefer one or the other. Circle the form you would be most likely to use. Be prepared to discuss your choices.

1. We (can't help but / must) wonder about the future.
2. He is one of those persons who (are / is) always worrying.
3. The king (only wanted / wanted only) a *little* butter.
4. We are not (as / so) confident about it as we used to be.
5. Two and two (are / is) four.
6. (All of / All) the men in my family are thin.
7. The group at the next table (are / is) ordering now.
8. There has been cooperation (among / between) the nations of the western hemisphere.
9. (The angle of the roof / The roof's angle) is too steep.
10. Have you heard about (him / his) winning the race?
11. The data (are / is) available for us to use.
12. (What did they ask about / About what did they ask)?
13. My answer is different (from / than / to) yours.
14. The game was called (because of / due to / owing to) darkness.
15. The members of the soccer team congratulated (each other / one another).
16. She decided not to drive any (farther / further) that day.
17. Do you know (if / whether) the movie has started yet?
18. The school has (fewer / less) students than last year.
19. The invitation was for my sister and (me / myself).
20. I hope (quickly to / to quickly) finish mowing the lawn.

1.9   Historical Varieties

DIRECTIONS   One kind of language variety results from the passage of time. Below are four versions of the Lord's Prayer. The translations were made about 1000, 1380, 1611, and 1974, but are not in chronological order. Compare the four versions to see how they differ.

A. Our father which art in heauen, hallowed be thy Name. Thy kingdome come. Thy will be done, in earth, as it is in heauen. Giue vs this day our dayly bread. And forgiue vs our debts, as we forgiue our debters. And leade vs not into temptation, but deliuer vs from euill: For thine is the kingdome, and the power, and the glory, for euer, Amen.

B. Fæder ure, þu þe eart on heofonum, si þin nama gehalgod. Tobecume þin rice. Gewurðe þin willa on eorðan swa swa on heofonum. Urne gedæg-hwamlican hlaf syle us to dæg. And forgyf us ure gyltas, swa swa we forgyfað urum gyltendum. And ne gelæd þu us on costnunge, ac alys us of yfele. Soðlice.

C. Oure fadir that art in heuenes halowid be thi name, thi kyngdom come to, be thi wille don in erthe as in heuene, yeue to us this day oure breed ouir other substaunce, & foryeue to us oure dettis, as we foryeuen to oure dettouris, & lede us not in to temptacion: but delyuer us from yuel, amen.

D. Our Father, who is in heaven, may your name be kept holy. May your kingdom come into being. May your will be followed on earth, just as it is in heaven. Give us this day our food for the day. And forgive us our offenses, just as we forgive those who have offended us. And do not bring us to the test. But free us from evil. For the kingdom, the power, and the glory are yours forever. Amen.

1. Match the letters of the translations with the dates:

   _____ 1000   _____1380   _____1611   _____1974

2. List several differences in spelling that may indicate a difference in pronunciation. _____

3. List several differences in vocabulary. _____

4. List several differences in grammar, such as word order. _____

   _____

1.10   Black English Nouns

DIRECTIONS   **Black English** is the term used for the variety of language spoken by many, though not all, black Americans. Many of the features of this variety are shared by whites, and blacks who use some form of the dialect differ in how consistent they are in its features.

Standard English has long used some nouns in a plural sense but without the usual form for the plural. Thus, *He's six feet tall* and *He's six foot tall* both occur, although the latter is apt to be restricted to informal contexts. Black English is quite systematic in the way it uses a plural noun sometimes with and sometimes without a distinctive plural form. Notice the form of the italicized nouns and the phrases in which they are used.

> He only paid ten *cent* apiece for the *books*.
> He'll loan two *dollar* to his *friends*.
> She kept the *dogs* for five *year*.
> She ain't walked three *mile* for *years*.

1. When does the noun have a distinct plural form, and when is it plural in sense without such a distinct form?

    _____

    _____

    _____

DIRECTIONS   The feature illustrated in the following sentences has no close parallel in standard English.

> That man house is over there.
> Paul brother drove the car.
> Give me you hand.
> They lost they pencil.
> I like that girl hair.

2. Describe the feature that distinguishes these sentences from standard English.

    _____

    _____

    _____

10

1.11   Omitted and Invariant BE

DIRECTIONS   In several varieties of English, including black English, forms of the verb BE can be omitted from some sentences. In addition, black English, in particular, sometimes uses an invariant form of BE: *I be, he be, they be.* The following sentences illustrate the omitted and the invariant BE:

OMITTED BE

> Woodbine, Georgia, it close to Jacksonville.
> Daddy say it dangerous over there.
> He kind of like a snake.
> They in the lake, them eel.
> His name Willie.
> My uncle works for the city; he a trashman.

INVARIANT BE

> Sometime he be on the ground.
> They got a free medical clinic down there where Grady doctors be at.
> Six or seven, that's when I be at home.
> I wear my coat sometime when it be raining.
> Mama say that while she [the baby] be laughing, some angels be making her laugh.
> Sometime she be wanting somebody to hold her.

The rules for these two kinds of BE are complex, and both have several uses; there is, however, a tendency to use them with the time meanings referred to below:†

1. Which kind of BE is used to refer to a permanent condition?

   _____

2. Which kind of BE is used to refer to a condition that is intermittent?

   _____

3. How would the following sentences differ in meaning?

   a. They in Macon. _____

   b. They be in Macon._____

4. Why might each of the following sentences be thought odd? (The star indicates that the sentence is ungrammatical.)

   a. *He be my brother. _____

   b. *Sometime he funny. _____

5. In what way can black English be more specific than other varieties of English in talking about the time of events? _____

   _____

---

† The complexities in the use of this verb are described by Howard G. Dunlap in "Social Aspects of a Verb Form: Native Atlanta Fifth-Grade Speech—the Present Tense of BE" (dissertation, Emory University, 1973), from which the sentences above are taken.

1.12   Indirect Question Patterns

DIRECTIONS   English has matching statements and questions like the following:

STATEMENT	QUESTION
They will go.	Will they go?
She could help.	Could she help?
It is ready.	Is it ready?
He can stop.	Can he stop?

There are, however, two ways of forming indirect questions (the sort that begin "They asked . . ." or the like). One kind of indirect question is that favored by standard English; the other is less common in standard use, but is favored in a number of dialects, including black English.

INDIRECT QUESTION 1	INDIRECT QUESTION 2
He wonders whether they will go.	He wonders will they go.
She asked if she could help.	She asked could she help.
Let me see whether it is ready.	Let me see is it ready.
I don't know if he can stop.	I don't know can he stop.

1. Describe the difference between the two forms of the indirect question.

    INDIRECT QUESTION 1: _____

    _____

    INDIRECT QUESTION 2: _____

    _____

2. Write the other indirect question that would correspond to each of these:

    a. Nobody asked me whether I would be there.

    _____

    b. Find out if everybody is finished.

    _____

    c. I wonder should we do that.

    _____

1.13 Conditions; Slang Vocabulary

DIRECTIONS   Examine the following black English sentences.† They share a characteristic that is sometimes used in standard English, but is more common in certain regional and social dialects.

People don't want to do it, then no sense getting mad about it.
You able to do it, just do it.
He can walk out, she can walk out.
She can do me some good, that's cool.
Somebody offered you one, would you take it?
She wanted proof, I could give her proof.

1. How does the structure of these sentences differ from the usual structure of standard English?

   _____

   _____

   _____

2. Rewrite the last sentence as it would usually be expressed in standard English.

   _____

DIRECTIONS   The most pronounced influence of black English on the standard language has been in vocabulary, especially slang. Words like *jazz* and *juke box* began as black slang but moved into general currency; most slang is ephemeral, but some of it survives and becomes widespread. The words below are, or have been, voguish terms in the conversation of many Americans and other English speakers, who may not be aware of their origin in the black community. Give a synonym for each of the terms that you are familiar with.

3. (one's) bag _____   9. nitty-gritty _____

4. boss (adj.) _____   10. out of sight _____

5. cat   _____   11. rap (verb)   _____

6. cop (verb) _____   12. strung-out   _____

7. dude   _____   13. tough   _____

8. hip (adj.) _____   14. uptight   _____

† Adapted from Elaine E. Tarone, "Aspects of Intonation in Black English," *American Speech,* in press.

1.14   Black English Exemplified

DIRECTIONS   The following passage is a variety of English spoken by an eleven-year-old boy whose father is a construction worker. Read the passage, note its distinctive features, and list as many of them as you can in the space below the passage.

We went fishing on the Fourth of July, and we had a big old picnic. . . . And this man—the dry-cleaning man what cleaning our clothes—he went with us too, cause Daddy and Mama, they're very good friends of him. And sometimes . . . on Saturday when he don't have to work, he come over to our house. He bring . . . us lobster and he bring us pork—pork chops and steaks and all that—all that stuff. And Mama just cook it on Sunday. And that plate, it— Mama have a big old plate, and it be full the next day. I be eating it—I be wanting some of that. Mama told me to wait till they get through. And Mushy, she— And my little sister named Sue—we call her Mushy, cause she's so bad—she come over there. . . . She act like she want to fill up off of meat. Mama said you can't fill up off of meat. Sometime you have to eat bread and stuff like that. [At the picnic] I et, and then I played games with my brother and them. Went back there—it's some tall trees over there, and we go up there —we play jungle man.†

---

† Adapted from Howard G. Dunlap, "Social Aspects of a Verb Form" (dissertation, Emory University, 1973), pp. 174–75.

14

● 2.1   Subject and Predicate

(Ref: CGCE 2.2)

DIRECTIONS   Most **sentences** can be divided into two parts: **subject** and **predicate.** Subjects can be recognized in several ways. (1) If the verb is the kind that changes its form to show the difference between singular and plural, the subject is the word or phrase it agrees with: *The cat hates water* but *The cats hate water.* (2) If a statement is changed into a question, the subject changes position with the verb: *The cat hates water* but *Does the cat hate water?* (3) The subject is often the theme of the sentence—what is being talked about—whereas the predicate is what is said about the subject: *The cat* [which is being discussed] *hates water* [what is said about it]. Divide the subject from the predicate with a line.

EXAMPLE   The old man carrying a cane **/** searched the room.

1. The dog / is burying a bone.
2. A gypsy moth / was flying around the candle flame.
3. The sound of crickets / can be very loud.
4. The banjo's string / twanged.
5. She / has knee-high boots on.
6. Mrs. O'Leary / is thinking about getting a cow.
7. The senator from Vermont / has been reelected.
8. Any man with a handlebar mustache / needs a special cup for coffee.
9. Papayas / don't grow in many parts of the world.
10. His brand-new sports car / broke an axle.

DIRECTIONS   Make up a subject or predicate, as needed to complete the sentence.

11. The man wearing a lumber jacket _____.
12. _____ slipped on a banana peel.
13. Anyone with a ticket for this performance _____.
14. _____ can climb out of a rock pit.
15. _____ are shaving their beards off.

2.2   Operators and Predications   (Ref: CGCE 2.2–3)

DIRECTIONS   Many predicates consist of two parts: the **operator,** which is the word that reverses position with the subject in questions, and the rest of the predicate, called the **predication.** Circle the word that serves or might serve as the operator, and underline the predication. (What is left will be the subject.)

EXAMPLES   It (was) raining.
          (Had) he given her an apple?

1. A scientist could study one subject for years.
2. Some scientists have studied the elementary particles of matter.
3. One physicist is writing a book about quarks.
4. Do you know about quarks?
5. They are supposed to be the basic building blocks of all matter.
6. Has anyone isolated a quark yet?
7. They might be recorded on photographs of cosmic rays.
8. Scientists must examine hundreds of thousands of photographs.
9. Will they find evidence of quarks?
10. No one can prove they exist.

DIRECTIONS   Rewrite each sentence, adding the potential operator given in parentheses. It will sometimes be necessary to change the form of the verb following the added word.

EXAMPLE   He gave her an apple.   (has)   **He has given her an apple.**

11. Oscar saw a falling star.   (has)   _____
12. They leave tomorrow.   (will)   _____
13. She plays the piano.   (is)   _____
14. The door opened quietly.   (has)   _____
15. The clouds blow away.   (may)   _____

2.3   Auxiliaries and the Operator

(Ref: CGCE 2.3–4)

DIRECTIONS   **Auxiliaries** are used with the **head verb** of a **verb phrase.** If there is more than one auxiliary, the first will serve as the operator. The head verb follows all auxiliaries and is the central word for the meaning of the verb phrase. Circle the actual or potential operator, and underline the other auxiliary or auxiliaries once and the head verb twice.

EXAMPLE   He (can) not have been questioned by the police.

1. The plane will be arriving soon.
2. We have been waiting for a long time.
3. They might have come by bus.
4. She could have been watching a movie.
5. She may have been detoured by the storm.
6. We were being served by the steward.
7. You would be missed by everyone.
8. It must have been raining.
9. Shall we be going now?
10. The room had been emptied suddenly.
11. He has been being bitten by mosquitos all day. [rare]
12. Should witnesses be being questioned during the recess? [rare]

DIRECTIONS   The head verbs of the following sentences have no auxiliaries. Rewrite each sentence, adding one or more auxiliaries and making any necessary changes in the form of the head verb. Circle the auxiliaries you have added.

EXAMPLE   It rained.   It (must have been) raining.

13. Supper cooked.   _____
14. Windows break.   _____
15. The wolf howls.   _____

2.4   Sentence Elements (1)   (Ref: CGCE 2.5)

DIRECTIONS   Another way of analyzing sentences is into **elements** such as **subject** (S), **verb** (V), **complement** (C), **object** (O), and **adverbial** (A). The object usually comes after the verb and usually refers to someone or something different from the subject: *John hired a lawyer* (the subject *John* and the object *a lawyer* are different persons). The complement also usually comes after the verb, but it always refers to the same person or thing as another element (in these sentences, the subject): *John became a lawyer* (the subject *John* and the complement *a lawyer* are the same person). Complements may also describe the subject: *John became happier* (the complement *happier* describes *John*). Adverbials can usually be moved about within the sentence: *He turned slowly. He slowly turned. Slowly he turned.* Identify the elements by writing the appropriate letter in the parentheses following each element.

EXAMPLES   Patricia (**S**) is studying (**V**) intently (**A**) now (**A**).

John (**S**) carefully (**A**) searched (**V**) the room (**O**).

The girl (**S**) is (**V**) a student (**C**) at the university (**A**).

1. Quasiland (   ) is (   ) a floating island (   ).
2. It (   ) drifts (   ) freely (   ) in the tide (   ).
3. The Sultan of Quasiland (   ) has ruled (   ) the island (   ) for many years (   ).
4. He (   ) married (   ) thirty-four wives (   ).
5. Recently (   ), the Sultan (   ) reluctantly (   ) decreed (   ) an austerity program (   ).
6. He (   ) consequently (   ) reduced (   ) the number of his wives (   ).
7. Now (   ) he (   ) has (   ) only ten (   ).
8. The Sultan (   ) feels (   ) deprived (   ).
9. He (   ) probably (   ) will seek (   ) foreign aid (   ) from a more stable nation (   ).
10. The island of Quasiland (   ) someday (   ) may become (   ) a great power (   ).

2.5   Objects and Complements (Ref: CGCE 2.6)

DIRECTIONS   An object may be either a **direct object** or an **indirect object.** If a sentence has only one object, it is direct; but if a sentence has both indirect and direct objects, the indirect object usually comes first and can be omitted or replaced by a phrase with *to* or *for: She sent her brother a letter. She sent a letter (to her brother).* A complement may be either a **subject complement** or an **object complement.** A subject complement refers to the subject: *He is a hero* (or *heroic*). An object complement refers to the direct object: *The danger made him a hero* (or *heroic*). Identify each italicized element as direct object (Od), indirect object (Oi), subject complement (Cs), or object complement (Co) by writing the appropriate abbreviation in the parentheses after it.

EXAMPLES   John searched *the room* (**Od**).

He gave *her* (**Oi**) *an apple* (**Od**).

His brother grew *happier* (**Cs**).

They made *him* (**Od**) *the chairman* (**Co**).

1. The treaty guaranteed *the Cherokees* (   ) *a hunting tract* (   ).

2. The Thistlebaums showed *us* (   ) *their home movies* (   ).

3. The dog is digging *a hole* (   ) in the garden.

4. Many amateur athletes are going *professional* (   ).

5. The team considered *the season* (   ) *a success* (   ).

6. Alex is becoming *a corporate lawyer* (   ).

7. On Saturdays, he watches *football* (   ) on television.

8. Television keeps *the children* (   ) *happy* (   ).

9. The postman brought *the old man* (   ) *a special delivery letter* (   ).

10. The minister pronounced *them* (   ) *man and wife* (   ).

11. You can smell *the fresh bread* (   ) in the bakery.

12. Freshly baked bread certainly smells *good* (   ).

2.6   Sentence Elements (2)   (Ref: CGCE 2.5–6)

DIRECTIONS   Identify each sentence element by writing the appropriate symbol in the parentheses after it: S, V, Od, Oi, Cs, Co, A. Some elements [enclosed in square brackets] themselves have the internal structure of sentences. Thus, in the last of the examples below, *that it was raining* is the object of the whole sentence, but includes a subject (*it*) and a verb (*was raining*).

EXAMPLES   He (**S**) had given (**V**) her (**Oi**) an apple (**Od**).

They (**S**) made (**V**) him (**Od**) treasurer (**Co**) last year (**A**).

His brother (**S**) gradually (**A**) grew (**V**) happier (**Cs**).

She (**S**) saw (**V**) that [it (**S**) was raining (**V**)] (**O**).

1. The waitress (   ) was pouring (   ) him (   ) a cup of coffee (   ).

2. The meeting (   ) unanimously (   ) elected (   ) her (   ) president (   ).

3. The weather (   ) unexpectedly (   ) turned (   ) bitter cold (   ).

4. That author (   ) probably (   ) is writing (   ) another novel (   ).

5. The clown (   ) was hiccupping (   ) uncontrollably (   ).

6. Team members (   ) must wear (   ) red blazers (   ) out of town (   ).

7. The politician's speech (   ) got (   ) the crowd (   ) angry (   ).

8. The Chief Justice of the Supreme Court (   ) gives (   ) the President (   ) the oath of office (   ).

9. The Archbishop of Canterbury (   ) crowns (   ) the heir (   ) King of England (   ).

10. Lightning (   ) was crackling (   ) all around the airplane (   ).

11. Huckleberry (   ) was hiding (   ) because [Aunt Sally (   ) was (   ) a terror (   )] (   ).

12. The politician (   ) told (   ) his audience (   ) that [he (   ) would serve (   ) them (   ) faithfully (   ) in Washington (   )] (   ).

13. That [men (   ) should have reached (   ) the moon (   )] (   ) is (   ) remarkable (   ).

14. The reason for his sudden departure (   ) was (   ) that [the police (   ) had discovered (   ) his fraud (   )] (   ).

2.7   Verb Categories: Intensive and Extensive   (Ref: CGCE 2.6–7)

DIRECTIONS   There are several categories of verbs: **intensive**, used with a subject complement (He *is* happy), and EXTENSIVE, which may be any of the following: **intransitive**, used with no complements or objects (It *rained*); **transitive**, used with a direct object (John *searched* the room); **ditransitive**, used with indirect and direct objects (He *gave* her an apple); and **complex transitive**, used with a direct object and object complement (They *made* him chairman). Identify the category of each italicized verb by writing the appropriate term in the blank. Use the five boldface terms.

EXAMPLE   Isaac finally *caught* a trout.   **transitive**

1. I never *promised* you a rose garden.   _____
2. The governor *proclaimed* tomorrow Dill Pickle Day. _____
3. The audience *seems* sleepy.   _____
4. Philanthropists sometimes *endow* universities. _____
5. The moon *shone* brightly.   _____
6. Albert *received* an unexpected long-distance call. _____
7. Scientists *have proven* the theory wrong.   _____
8. The millionaire *left* each child a fortune.   _____
9. The squirrel *became* a pet.   _____
10. The leaves slowly *floated* downward.   _____

DIRECTIONS   Write a sentence using each verb in the category specified.

11. drink (intransitive) _____
12. drink (transitive) _____
13. wash (transitive) _____
14. wash (complex transitive) _____
15. get (intensive) _____
16. get (ditransitive) _____

2.8 Verb Categories: Dynamic and Stative   (Ref: CGCE 2.8)

DIRECTIONS   **Dynamic verbs** can be freely used in the progressive form (ending in -*ing*): He *learned* (or *was learning*) the answers. **Stative verbs** are seldom progressive: He *knew* (not **was knowing*) the answers. If the italicized verb is dynamic, rewrite it in the progressive form, and mark the sentence *D;* if it is stative, mark the sentence *S.*

EXAMPLES   It *rained* all day.   <u>was raining   D</u>

           She *is* tall.   <u>   S</u>

1. He *seemed* well-informed. _____
2. He *became* well-informed. _____
3. Angela *had* a cold. _____
4. Angela *caught* a cold. _____
5. Morgan *eats* ketchup on everything. _____
6. Morgan *likes* ketchup on everything. _____
7. We *saw* the eclipse yesterday. _____
8. We *watched* the eclipse yesterday. _____
9. Eloise *imitates* her mother. _____
10. Eloise *resembles* her mother. _____

DIRECTIONS   *Quickly, gradually, accidentally, deliberately, sparingly, avidly, carefully, carelessly, expertly,* and *amateurishly* are examples of **process adverbials,** which are used with dynamic verbs, but normally not with stative verbs. Rewrite the sentences above that have dynamic verbs, adding one of the foregoing process adverbials to each.

11. _____
12. _____
13. _____
14. _____
15. _____

2.9   Categories of Adverbial   (Ref: CGCE 2.9)

DIRECTIONS   Three categories of adverbial are those of **time,** of **place,** and of **process.** Underline each adverbial and indicate what category it belongs to.

EXAMPLES   She is studying Swahili <u>now</u>. _____ **time** _____

   She is studying Swahili <u>eagerly</u>. _____ **process** _____

   She is studying Swahili <u>at a large university</u>. _____ **place** _____

1. Charlie Brown lost another game yesterday.   _____

2. Albert hid his diary in a drawer.   _____

3. Coretta opened the door determinedly.   _____

4. The airplane taxied onto the runway.   _____

5. Then the pilot gunned the motor.   _____

6. The tower suddenly gave the all-clear signal.   _____

7. The game ended before nine.   _____

8. The fans left with glee.   _____

9. The team was celebrating in the locker room.   _____

10. The paperboy left a newspaper here.   _____

DIRECTIONS   *Now* is a typical adverbial of time; *here*, of place; and *eagerly*, of process. In some of the blanks below, only one of the typical adverbials will fit easily; in other blanks, either of two adverbials might be used; and in one of the blanks, any of the three adverbials is possible. In each blank, write as many of the three adverbials as readily fit.

11. Molly _____ reads the newspaper.

12. Molly is _____.

13. Molly reads the newspaper _____.

14. Molly has a friend _____.

15. Molly reads the newspaper very _____.

2.10   Types of Sentence Structure

(Ref: CGCE 2.10)

DIRECTIONS   From the word categories and sentence elements introduced so far, eight basic sentence types can be constructed, each with some optional adverbials:

1. S V-*stat* A-*place:* She is in London (now).
2. S V-*stat* Cs: She is a student (in London) (now).
3. S V-*stat* Od: John heard the explosion (from his office) (as he locked the door).
4. S V-*dyn* Cs: Universities (gradually) became famous (in Europe) (during the Middle Ages).
5. S V-*dyn* Od: They ate the meat (hungrily) (in their hut) (that night).
6. S V-*dyn* Oi Od: He (politely) offered her an apple (outside the hall) (before the concert).
7. S V-*dyn* Od Co: They elected him chairman (without argument) (in Washington) (this morning).
8. S V-*dyn:* The train arrived (quietly) (at the station) (before we noticed it).

Indicate the basic type of each sentence by writing the number of the type in the blank. Rewrite each, adding as many kinds of optional adverbials as possible.

EXAMPLE   He polished the teapot.   5

He polished the teapot eagerly in the kitchen yesterday.

1. Agnes was outside.   _____

2. The judges voted her queen.   _____

3. The nutcracker broke.   _____

4. Someone sent them an invitation.   _____

5. She preferred mustard.   _____

6. A tornado demolished many houses.   _____

7. We got ready.   _____

8. The weather seems pleasant.   _____

2.11   Parts of Speech   (Ref: CGCE 2.11–16)

DIRECTIONS   Words are classified as **parts of speech** (**noun, pronoun, verb, adjective, article, adverb, preposition, conjunction, interjection**) according to their use in sentences. Circle the words after each sentence that could fill the blank in it, and write the name of their part of speech in the blank on the right.

1. John has a _____.   _____
   question   never   room   lengthen   sister

2. He prefers the _____ one.   _____
   large   endow   quickly   beautiful   round

3. Ellen did it _____.   _____
   room   quickly   then   pencil   steadily

4. They _____ it.   _____
   large   searched   very   grow   like

5. _____ did that.   _____
   He   Somebody   They   New   Tree

6. He put it _____ the box.   _____
   walk   in   under   near   quickly

7. He left _____ she stayed.   _____
   near   and   although   they   but

8. "_____," he said, "it's gone!"   _____
   In   Room   Oh   Ugh   Damn

9. George drove _____ new car.   _____
   the   a   but   of   when

DIRECTIONS   If a part of speech has a large number of members and can freely add new ones, it is an **open class**; if it has few members and resists new additions, it is a **closed system**. Which of the parts of speech illustrated above are open classes and which closed systems?

10. Open classes: _____

11. Closed systems: _____

2.12 Types of Structure (1) (Ref: CGCE 2.11–16)

DIRECTIONS A **noun phrase** (NP), **verb phrase** (VP), **adjective phrase** (AjP), or **adverb phrase** (AvP) is a group of words that has as its **head word** a noun, verb, adjective, or adverb, respectively. Identify the type of each phrase by writing the appropriate symbol in the blank, and circle the head word.

EXAMPLE   the new (stove)   **NP**

1. ten fat blackbirds   _____

2. have been being watched   _____

3. far too carelessly   _____

4. very much quieter   _____

5. will be exploring   _____

6. not quite eagerly   _____

7. much too good   _____

8. almost enough coffee   _____

9. both the next boats   _____

10. might have experimented   _____

DIRECTIONS Each of the following sentences is made up of three phrases. Divide the phrases from one another with slashes and identify the type of each phrase.

EXAMPLE   The old man / was reading / the morning paper.   **NP / VP / NP**

11. An angry chipmunk is scolding the cats.   _____

12. The acrobat has been getting much more skillful. _____

13. Very suddenly, the train had stopped.   _____

14. The French student can speak very fluently.   _____

15. The latest news may seem altogether unbelievable. _____

2.13 Realization of Verb Elements (Ref: CGCE 2.11)

DIRECTIONS   Verb phrases are either finite or nonfinite. A **finite verb phrase** can be used as the verb element of an independent sentence: *has been watching* as in *He has been watching television.* A **nonfinite verb phrase** cannot be used as the only verb of an independent sentence: *having watched* as in *Having watched television, he went to bed,* in which the verb element of the sentence is *went.* Write each verb phrase in a blank on the right and mark it *F* if it is finite, *N* if it is nonfinite.

EXAMPLES	Mary has gone to the university.	has gone F
	Mary wanted to go to the university.	wanted F
		to go N

1. The fish are biting today. _____

2. Suddenly, a balloon popped. _____

3. George has joined the Navy. _____

4. We are hoping to see a good show. _____

   _____

5. Making popcorn seemed like a good idea. _____

   _____

6. Given a choice, most people would prefer peanuts. _____

   _____

7. The fishermen were leaving, having caught the limit. _____

   _____

8. He has been studying Hebrew because he is going to Israel. _____

   _____

9. It had seemed important for him to learn the language like a native. _____

   _____

10. The quarterback was carried out of the stadium, his arm broken. _____

    _____

2.14 Types of Structure (2)

(Ref: CGCE 2.11–16)

DIRECTIONS A **prepositional phrase** (PP) consists of a preposition and a noun phrase (for example, *at* + *a large university*, as in *She studied at a large university*). **Clauses** consist of the sentence elements S, V, O, C, and A, but may be either finite or nonfinite. A **finite clause** (FC) has a finite verb phrase for its verb element, whereas a **nonfinite clause** (NFC) has a nonfinite verb phrase.

FINITE CLAUSE: after he *had been watching* television

NONFINITE CLAUSE: after *having watched* television

Identify the type of each structure by writing the appropriate symbol in the blank. Then circle the preposition, finite verb phrase, or nonfinite verb phrase, as appropriate.

EXAMPLE (to be watching) television   **NFC**

1. behind the next house   _____

2. when the music stopped   _____

3. having sent his family a postcard   _____

4. driving an entry in the Grand Prix   _____

5. what everyone was hoping   _____

6. after a brief pause   _____

DIRECTIONS The same idea can sometimes be expressed by a prepositional phrase, finite clause, or nonfinite clause. Identify the type of each italicized structure; then phrase it another way.

EXAMPLE He watched television *after dinner*.   **PP**

   after he had dinner (FC) *or* after having dinner (NFC)

7. Olga studied *before the test*.   _____

   _____

8. She played a tape recorder *while she slept*.   _____

   _____

2.15   Realization of Other Sentence Elements   (Ref: CGCE 2.11)

DIRECTIONS   Put parentheses around the subject and objects of the main sentence and indicate whether each is an *NP* (noun phrase, noun, or pronoun), *FC* (finite clause), or *NFC* (nonfinite clause) by writing the appropriate symbols in the blanks.

EXAMPLE   (He) gave (the girl) (what she wanted).   <u>NP</u>   <u>NP</u>   <u>FC</u>

1. Olly met the jolly green giant.   ____   ____
2. He discovered that vegetables are good for you.   ____   ____
3. Weeding the garden exhausted Stan.   ____   ____
4. You can show me how to get there.   ____   ____   ____
5. The old woman asked us how we were.   ____   ____   ____

DIRECTIONS   Put parentheses around each complement, and indicate whether it is an *AjP* (adjective phrase or adjective), *NP*, *FC*, or *NFC*.

6. His novels seem very skillful.   _____
7. Transylvania may become a great world power.   _____
8. Her hobby is collecting wine bottles.   _____
9. A good reporter stays alert.   _____
10. The fact is that no animal can talk.   _____

DIRECTIONS   Put parentheses around each adverbial and indicate whether it is an *AvP* (adverb phrase or adverb), *PP* (prepositional phrase), *NP*, *FC*, or *NFC*.

11. The diplomat was stationed in Lima.   _____
12. The detective casually pocketed the revolver.   _____
13. We closed the window because it was raining.   _____
14. He wears lifts to look taller.   _____
15. He is leaving here next week.   _____   _____
16. Mrs. Golightly almost always chairs the meeting.   _____
17. Having lost ten straight games, the pitcher was traded.   _____

2.16   Pro-Forms

(Ref: CGCE 2.17)

DIRECTIONS   A **pro-form** is an expression used in place of a noun, noun phrase, verb phrase, clause, or the like. Put parentheses around the word or words that each italicized pro-form replaces.

EXAMPLE   John left (the big room) after he had searched *it.*

1. After Wolfie had bitten into the green apple, he discovered a worm in *it.*
2. After Wolfie had bitted into the green apple, *he* discovered a worm in it.
3. As soon as he sells his old car, he plans to buy a new *one.*
4. We will be studying at the library, so you can find us *there.*
5. Alice isn't available on Mondays, because she takes karate *then.*
6. Felicia is relaxed, but Arlene is even more *so.*
7. Throckmorton is into judo, and *so* is Chumley.
8. Zenobia promised she would paint the house and she did *so.*
9. I think that she has finished painting; I hope *so.*
10. We haven't been reading mystery novels, and he *hasn't* either.
11. Pearlie May has been playing the classical guitar for three years, *hasn't* she?
12. I am beginning to read "War and Peace," and Phil *is* too.

DIRECTIONS   Fill the blank with an appropriate pro-form to replace the italicized expression.

13. The fat *man* and the thin _____ both liked the tattooed lady.
14. The lion-tamer exercised *his cats* and fed _____ every evening.
15. *The India rubber man* could tie _____ in knots.
16. My cousin is living *in Bermuda,* so we are going to visit her _____.
17. Albert is *fond of waterskiing,* and _____ is Marty.
18. We *should be careful not to swim near sharks,* _____n't we?
19. Throckmorton wants to *study kung fu* and intends to _____.
20. Chumley says *that he is a chess master,* and I believe _____.

2.17 *Wh-* Questions

(Ref: CGCE 2.18)

DIRECTIONS   For each of the following statements, write a corresponding *wh-* question that asks for an identification of the italicized expression. Begin the question with *who, whose, whom, what, which, when, where, why,* or *how.*

EXAMPLE   Mary is *in London.*   **Where is Mary?**

1. *Hazel Pentecott* can read palms.

_____

2. She told Milton *that he was going on a trip.*

_____

3. She is going to read *Albert's* palm next.

_____

4. *This* line tells whether you will marry.

_____

5. Hazel reads palms *for fun.*

_____

6. Hazel will read palms for *anyone who asks her.*

_____

7. Hazel does her best palm-reading *at midnight.*

_____

8. She learned the art *by studying with a gypsy.*

_____

9. The head line is *between the heart and life lines.*

_____

10. Hazel talked about *her gypsy teacher.*

_____

11. If you offer her both palms, she prefers to read *the right.*

_____

2.18 *Yes-No Questions*

DIRECTIONS   For each of the following statements, write a corresponding *yes-no* question (one that can be answered with *yes* or *no*).

EXAMPLE   The girl is a student now.   **Is the girl a student now?**

1. The cat is chasing a squirrel.

_____

2. Enoch has decided to study kung fu.

_____

3. The milkman should have left buttermilk.

_____

4. There could be a rock slide on the mountain.

_____

5. The car door locked automatically.

_____

6. The stairs creak when you step on them.

_____

7. The Canary Islands are in the Eastern Hemisphere.

_____

8. A band of pirates might have landed there.

_____

9. Treasure hunters have been searching the island.

_____

10. Huck has a wart on his thumb.

_____

11. The man carrying the alligator bag would be Albert.

_____

2.19   Negation and Nonassertion

(Ref: CGCE 2.20)

DIRECTIONS   For each of the following **assertions**, write three corresponding **nonassertions**: a) a **negative statement**, b) a **positive question**, and c) a **negative question**.

EXAMPLE   He offered her some chocolates.

a. **He didn't offer her any chocolates.**

b. **Did he offer her any chocolates?**

c. **Didn't he offer her any chocolates?**

1. Miriam told them a story.

   a. _____

   b. _____

   c. _____

2. Jonathan was David's son.

   a. _____

   b. _____

   c. _____

3. Scientists have discovered life on Mars.

   a. _____

   b. _____

   c. _____

4. The rocket will take off tomorrow.

   a. _____

   b. _____

   c. _____

5. There should be a problem.

   a. _____

   b. _____

   c. _____

● **3.1 Types of Verb** (Ref: CGCE 3.1, App I.18)

DIRECTIONS   Verbs are either lexical or auxiliary. A **lexical verb** is the head of a verb phrase. An **auxiliary verb** is used with a lexical verb and can serve as the operator. They are either **primary auxiliaries** (*be, have, do*) or **modal auxiliaries** (*will, shall, can, may,* etc.). Indicate whether each italicized verb is lexical (L) or auxiliary (A) by writing the appropriate letter in the parentheses.

EXAMPLE   They *might* (**A**) *be* (**A**) *fishing* (**L**) in the creek.

1. We *have* (   ) never *baked* (   ) bread before.
2. The oven *is* (   ) *heating* (   ).
3. The dough *has* (   ) *been* (   ) *rising* (   ) all morning.
4. *Shall* (   ) we *dance* (   )?
5. The door *must* (   ) *be* (   ) *locked* (   ).
6. The swallows *may* (   ) *come* (   ) back to Capistrano.
7. Orson *could* (   ) *sell* (   ) refrigerators to Eskimos.
8. *Can* (   ) you *can* (   ) rhubarb?
9. I *will* (   ) *will* (   ) my fortune to charity.
10. He *does* (   ) not *do* (   ) that for a living.
11. Ludwig *ought* (   ) to *get* (   ) a toupee.
12. *Dare* (   ) he *eat* (   ) a peach?

DIRECTIONS   Some lexical verbs have suffixes that help to identify their part of speech. Write the suffix that ends each verb.

EXAMPLE   simplify   **-ify**

13. hyphenate _____
14. purify   _____
15. symbolize _____
16. flicker   _____
17. sparkle _____
18. moisten _____
19. solidify _____
20. sniffle _____
21. moralize   _____
22. chatter   _____
23. sicken   _____
24. assassinate _____

3.2 Verbal Forms

DIRECTIONS Most English verbs have five forms: the **base** *drink, call* (V); **-s form** *drinks, calls* (V-s); **past** *drank, called* (V-ed₁); **-ing participle** *drinking, calling* (V-ing); and **-ed participle** *drunk, called* (V-ed₂). Identify the form of each italicized verb by writing the appropriate symbol in the parentheses.

EXAMPLE They *called* (**V-ed₁**) every day.

1. Orangutans *live* (   ) in Borneo and Sumatra.   2. The word "orangutan," *meaning* (   ) 'forest man,' *comes* (   ) from the Malay language.   3. Nowadays orangutans are *restricted* (   ) to swampy forests on the islands, but they used to *live* (   ) also on the mainland of Asia. 4. *Related* (   ) to the gorilla and chimpanzee, the orangutan *resembles* (   ) them but *has* (   ) shaggy red hair.   5. If you *visit* (   ) the forests, you can *see* (   ) orangs that are *making* (   ) platforms from branches.   6. After he has *made* (   ) a platform, the orang will *lie* (   ) down and *cover* (   ) himself with leaves.   7. The eighteenth-century jurist Lord Monboddo *believed* (   ) that the orangs *were* (   ) primitive men who had never *learned* (   ) to *talk* (   ).

DIRECTIONS Each auxiliary determines the form of the verb that follows it: *be* requires that it be one of the participles; *have,* that it be an *-ed* participle; and *do* and the modals, that it be a base form. Make a verb phrase out of each group of verbs.

EXAMPLE should, be, watch _____**should be watching *or* should be watched**_____

8. have, try _____
9. be, think _____
10. do, hurry _____
11. will, finish _____

12. have, be, cook _____
13. would, have, show _____
14. ought to, be, see _____
15. be, be, entertain _____

3.3   Regular Lexical Verbs   (Ref: CGCE 3.3–4)

DIRECTIONS   The past and the *-ed* participle forms of **regular verbs** are identical. Write the inflected forms of each of the following regular verbs.

EXAMPLE call	**calling**	**calls**	**called**
BASE	*-ing* PARTICIPLE	*-s* FORM	PAST/*-ed* PARTICIPLE
1. laugh			
2. steam			
3. test			
4. pack			
5. play			

DIRECTIONS   The *-s* form and the *-ing* participle are regular for almost all verbs. There are, however, a handful of irregularities. Answer the questions about verbs with irregular *-s* or *-ing* forms.

6. *Be* is the most irregular verb in English. Write its *-s* form._____

7. The *-s* form of *have* is also irregular. Write it. _____

8. Write the *-s* form of *do*. _____ How is it irregular in pronunciation?
_____

9. Write the *-s* form of *go*._____ Is it also irregular in pronunciation?
_____

10. Write the *-s* form of *say*. _____ Its spelling is regular, but its pronunciation is not. How is the latter irregular? _____
_____

11. The word *lightning* is sometimes used as a verb, as in *It lightninged a lot last night*. What is the *-ing* participle as it would be used in a sentence like the following? *It is* _____ *a lot right now.*

3.4 Pronouncing the -s and -ed Forms   (Ref: CGCE 3.5–6)

DIRECTIONS   The ending of the -s form is regularly pronounced in one of three ways: /s/, /z/, and /ɪz/ (or /əz/). How is the ending pronounced in each of the following verbs? Write the appropriate sound symbol after each.

EXAMPLE   passes   /ɪz/   calls   /z/   cuts   /s/

1. wishes _____	8. fans _____	15. likes _____
2. brags _____	9. taps _____	16. rubs _____
3. roars _____	10. itches _____	17. dims _____
4. misses _____	11. smooths _____	18. coughs _____
5. curves _____	12. puts _____	19. bids _____
6. frees _____	13. merges _____	20. pulls _____
7. quizzes _____	14. sings _____	21. unearths _____

DIRECTIONS   The ending of the past and -ed participle of regular verbs is also pronounced in one of three ways: /t/, /d/, and /ɪd/ (or /əd/). How is the ending pronounced in each of the following verbs? Write the appropriate sound symbol after each.

EXAMPLE   padded   /ɪd/   mowed   /d/   passed   /t/

22. heated _____	30. liked _____	38. pulled _____
23. bragged _____	31. folded _____	39. breathed _____
24. dimmed _____	32. curved _____	40. wished _____
25. hunted _____	33. itched _____	41. freed _____
26. rubbed _____	34. coughed _____	42. wronged _____
27. tapped _____	35. tested _____	43. roared _____
28. loaded _____	36. missed _____	44. gained _____
29. merged _____	37. quizzed _____	45. unearthed _____

3.5   Spelling Verbal Forms   (Ref: CGCE 3.5–9)

DIRECTIONS   The general spelling rules for suffixes apply also to the inflected forms of verbs. In addition, a few verbs have special rules for their spelling. Spell the inflected forms of the following verbs.

EXAMPLE push	pushes	pushing	pushed
BASE	-s FORM	-ing FORM	PAST/-ed PARTICIPLE
1. battle			
2. pass			
3. itch			
4. wish			
5. tax			
6. gossip			
7. plan			
8. tap			
9. look			
10. quiz			
11. picnic			
12. try			
13. merge			
14. tie			
15. hurry			
16. pay			
17. free			
18. dye			
19. shoe			
20. singe			
21. control			

3.6   Irregular Lexical Verbs

(Ref: CGCE 3.10–17)

DIRECTIONS   **Irregular verbs** form their past and *-ed* participle in some way other than by the regular addition of the /d, t, ɪd/ ending. Write the past and *-ed* participle of each of the following.

EXAMPLE   drink   ___**drank**___   ___**drunk**___

BASE	PAST	*-ed* PARTICIPLE
1. send		
2. make		
3. have		
4. leave		
5. buy		
6. tell		
7. let		
8. meet		
9. spin		
10. slide		
11. stand		
12. speak		
13. grow		
14. go		
15. sing		
16. run		
17. do		
18. lie (recline)		
19. ride		
20. flee		
21. show		
22. say		

3.7   Auxiliary Verbs

(Ref: CGCE 3.18–22)

DIRECTIONS   All the **auxiliaries** permit *not* to contract with them, and some of the auxiliaries can themselves contract with the subject. Underline the words that can contract and write the contractions in the blanks. If two contractions are possible, write both.

EXAMPLE   They <u>are</u> <u>not</u> going.   they're,   aren't

1. Do not they have bathtub races anymore?   _____

2. I have not seen one for years.   _____

3. It is not difficult to build a tub car.   _____

4. Tub cars cannot travel very fast.   _____

5. Should not a tub car be made from a real bathtub?   _____

6. I had been watching a race.   _____

7. I would rather see it on TV.   _____

8. They will not have a race this year.   _____

9. It did not bother us.   _____

10. We are not sure about it.   _____

11. I am not ready yet.   _____

DIRECTIONS   Some contractions are less common than others. What are the contractions of each of the following?

12. may not   _____   15. used not to _____

13. might not   _____   16. need not   _____

14. shall not   _____   17. dare not   _____

18. Look up the contraction *ain't* in several recent dictionaries. What do they say about the use of the form? _____

_____

3.8 Finite and Nonfinite Verb Phrases (Ref: CGCE 3.23)

DIRECTIONS A **finite verb phrase** can be used as the verb of an independent sentence; it usually begins with a verb in the present or past tense. A **nonfinite verb phrase** cannot be the verb of an independent sentence; it begins with an infinitive or a participle. Indicate whether the italicized verb phrases are finite (F) or nonfinite (N) by writing the appropriate letter in the parentheses.

EXAMPLE *To drive* (**N**) like that *must be* (**F**) dangerous.

1. Pigeons *will be nesting* (   ) on the statue's head.
2. After *hovering* (   ) overhead, the helicopter suddenly *descended* (   ).
3. *Having settled* (   ) into the chair, the cat *was beginning* (   ) *to wash* (   ) himself.
4. The house *had been painted* (   ) a bright red before it *was sold* (   ).
5. It *is* (   ) good *to have seen* (   ) the circus *being dismantled* (   ).
6. Murphy, *beaten* (   ) by the challenger, *has retired* (   ) from the ring.
7. *To be followed* (   ) all day *would make* (   ) anyone suspicious.

DIRECTIONS Rewrite each sentence, omitting the words in parentheses and changing the italicized finite verb phrase into a nonfinite verb phrase.

EXAMPLE While (he) *was eating*, he read the paper.

While eating, he read the paper.

8. (When she) *had signed* the letter, she mailed it.

_____

9. (Because he) *was overcome* by grief, he sat speechless.

_____

10. Before (they) *answered*, they thought carefully about the question.

_____

3.9   Tense, Aspect, and Voice   (Ref: CGCE 3.24–27)

DIRECTIONS   English verbs have two **tenses** (**present** and **past**) and three **aspects** (**simple, perfective,** and **progressive**) that join to produce eight tense-aspect combinations for finite verbs in the **active voice:**

	SIMPLE	PERFECTIVE	PROGRESSIVE	PERFECT-PROGRESSIVE
PRESENT	write(s)	have/has written	am/is/are writing	have/has been writing
PAST	wrote	had written	was/were writing	had been writing

1. The perfective is made with a form of the primary auxiliary HAVE + _____
   _____ (what form of the next verb?).

2. The progressive is made with a form of the primary auxiliary BE + _____
   _____ (what form of the next verb?).

3. When the progressive and the perfective are found in the same verb
   phrase, in what order do they come? _____

4. Write the eight tense-aspect combinations for *watch*:

PRESENT   _____   _____   _____   _____

PAST   _____   _____   _____   _____

DIRECTIONS   The same eight tense-aspect combinations occur in the **passive voice** of finite verbs:

	SIMPLE	PERFECTIVE	PROGRESSIVE	PERFECT-PROGRESSIVE
PRESENT	am/is/are written	have/has been written	am/is/are being written	have/has been being written
PAST	was/were written	had been written	was/were being written	had been being written

5. The passive is made with a form of the primary auxiliary BE + _____
   _____ (what form of the next verb?).

6. When the passive is found in the same verb phrase with the progressive or
   the perfective, in what order do they come? _____

7. Write the eight passive tense-aspect combinations for *watch*:

PRESENT   _____   _____   _____   _____

PAST   _____   _____   _____   _____

3.10   Aspect, Voice, and Mood   (Ref: CGCE 3.24–27)

DIRECTIONS   There are eight combinations of a **modal auxiliary** with the aspect auxiliaries, four in the active voice and four in the passive. *Would* is used here as a typical modal, though any of the others could replace it.

	SIMPLE	PERFECTIVE	PROGRESSIVE	PERFECT-PROGRESSIVE
ACTIVE	would write	would have written	would be writing	would have been writing
PASSIVE	would be written	would have been written	would be being written	would have been being written

1. The modal form is made with a modal + _____ (what form of the next verb?).

2. When a modal is found in the same verb phrase with the perfective, progressive, or passive, in what order do they come? _____
   _____

3. Write the eight modal-aspect-voice combinations for *watch:*

ACTIVE   _____   _____   _____   _____

PASSIVE   _____   _____   _____   _____

DIRECTIONS   **Nonfinite verb phrases** are either infinitive or participial. There are four active **infinitive phrases** and four passive:

	SIMPLE	PERFECTIVE	PROGRESSIVE	PERFECT-PROGRESSIVE
ACTIVE	(to) write	(to) have written	(to) be writing	(to) have been writing
PASSIVE	(to) be written	(to) have been written	(to) be being written	(to) have been being written

4. Write the eight infinitive phrases for *watch:*

ACTIVE   _____   _____   _____   _____

PASSIVE   _____   _____   _____   _____

DIRECTIONS   There are three active *-ing* **participial phrases** and three passive:

	SIMPLE	PERFECTIVE	PERFECTIVE-PROGRESSIVE
ACTIVE	writing	having written	having been writing
PASSIVE	being written	having been written	having been being written

5. Write the six *-ing* participial phrases for *watch:*

ACTIVE   _____   _____   _____

PASSIVE   _____   _____   _____

3.11   Present Time

(Ref: CGCE 3.28)

DIRECTIONS   An action in **present time** can be expressed by the simple present tense or by the present progressive, and it can be of three types: **timeless** (indicating habitual action or universal truths), **limited** (indicating an action in progress and of limited duration), or **instantaneous** (indicating an action more or less simultaneous with the statement that comments on it). Which of the three types of present time is expressed by each of the italicized verb phrases?

EXAMPLES   I always *write* with a special pen.   timeless

Today I *am writing* with a special pen.   limited

Watch carefully: now I *write* with pencil.   instantaneous

1. They *play* the national anthem at every game.   _____

2. Sylvia *is studying* Transcendental Meditation now.   _____

3. Now Lenski *breaks* away and *tries* for the down.   _____

4. Watch: we *brown* the onions and *add* garlic.   _____

5. The cats *are* forever *scratching* the furniture.   _____

6. Rose *is* busily *making* kreplach for supper.   _____

7. Spring *follows* winter every year.   _____

8. I now *pronounce* you man and wife.   _____

9. Herman *is reading* "The Circus Animals' Desertion."   _____

DIRECTIONS   What difference of meaning (if any) is implied by the choice of one verb or the other in these sentences?

10. They *put/are putting* sugar on their grapefruit before they eat it.

_____

11. I *put/am putting* the pea under one of the three shells before mixing them up. _____

12. That child continually *puts/is putting* his dirty hands on everything.

_____

3.12   Past Time

(Ref: CGCE 3.29–34)

DIRECTIONS   An action in past time can be expressed by several tense-aspect combinations: (1) **simple present,** the "historic present," used to create a sense of immediacy; (2) **simple past,** used for an event that took place in the past and is regarded as completed; (3) **present perfect,** used for a past event that has some relevance for the present and may still be in progress; (4) **past perfect,** used for a past event that had some relevance for a particular time in the past and may have continued until that time; (5) **past progressive,** used for an incomplete action of limited duration in the past; (6) **present perfect progressive,** used for a past event of incomplete or limited duration with relevance for the present; and (7) **past perfect progressive,** used for a past event of incomplete or limited duration with relevance for a particular time in the past. Identify the tense and aspect of each italicized verb phrase, and be prepared to explain why that tense-aspect combination was used and whether any other form might have been used instead.

EXAMPLE   I *have written* with a special pen since 1972.   _____**present perfect**_____

1. Albert *dropped* a coin into the well.   _____

2. Harry *has worked* for the city since last summer.   _____

3. We *were studying* at the library last night.   _____

4. Yesterday this man *calls* and *asks* for Mabel.   _____

5. I *have eaten* jellyfish before.   _____

6. Mac *had played* the tuba until he started piano.   _____

7. By the time Alex finished the dishes, he *had broken* three glasses.   _____

8. We *have been going* to Nassau every summer for ten years.   _____

9. The blackbirds *had been eating* the berries until we set out a scarecrow.   _____

10. Gwen *has been studying* French since last June.   _____

3.13 Verbal Meaning and the Progressive (Ref: CGCE 3.35)

DIRECTIONS **Dynamic verbs** are those that freely allow the progressive (*watch, is watching*); **stative verbs** are those that do not (*know, °is knowing*). Some verbs have both stative and dynamic uses (*see* 'perceive with the eyes,' *is seeing* 'is meeting with'). If the italicized verb is dynamic, write its progressive form in the blank and mark it *D*. If it is stative, write S in the blank.

EXAMPLES He *asked* a question.   <u>was asking   D</u>

He *disliked* spinach.   <u>   S   </u>

1. Herman *whispered* a secret.   _____
2. The crack in the ceiling *widened*.   _____
3. The dress *fit* her perfectly.   _____
4. His scalp *tingled* with fright.   _____
5. Myrtle *preferred* honey on her biscuits.   _____
6. Willis *heard* the bell.   _____
7. I *heard* about their trip.   _____
8. Huck *had* a plan.   _____
9. Huck *had* a good time.   _____
10. The plane *landed* at the airport.   _____
11. The law *applied* to everyone.   _____
12. Phil *applied* for a job.   _____

DIRECTIONS For each of the following verbs, write a sentence using the verb statively or dynamically, as indicated.

13. mind (stative)   _____
14. kick (dynamic)   _____
15. remain (stative)   _____
16. remain (dynamic)   _____

3.14   Future Time

(Ref: CGCE 3.36–44)

DIRECTIONS   **Future time** is expressed by various combinations of tense, aspect, and modality. Underline every verb phrase that refers to the future and identify the part of the verb phrase or any other expression in the sentence that signals the future time.

EXAMPLE   I will arrive tomorrow.   **will;   tomorrow**

1. We shall overcome.   _____

2. I'll tell you the truth.   _____

3. The trainer is going to put his head in the lion's mouth.   _____

4. Eli is playing in the next tournament.   _____

5. The race will be held if the weather clears.   _____

6. The astronauts lift off at noon tomorrow.   _____

7. The actors will be rehearsing then.   _____

8. The judge is to pass sentence on the prisoner.   _____

9. A strange dog is about to bite the mailman.   _____

DIRECTIONS   Underline the verb phrases that express time that is future from a viewpoint in the past. Identify the signals of future time.

10. He was going to lend me his notes.   _____

11. We were leaving on the following day.   _____

12. The witness was about to tell the truth.   _____

13. They were to meet at the Mall.   _____

3.15   The Subjunctive Mood   (Ref: CGCE 3.45–47)

DIRECTIONS   The **subjunctive** is a use of the base form of a verb either after certain verbs and adjectives to express a requirement (**mandative subjunctive**) or in set expressions (**formulaic subjunctive**). It may also be a use of the past form (especially the **subjunctive *were***) to indicate a condition that is contrary to fact. Underline the subjunctive verb in each sentence.

EXAMPLES   It is necessary that he <u>inform</u> himself.

<u>Come</u> what may, we will go ahead.

He spoke to me as if I <u>were</u> deaf.

1. I move that the chairman appoint a committee.
2. It is important that everyone be on time.
3. So be it.
4. God bless us, every one.
5. If today were Saturday, the stores would be open late.
6. He acted as though he were interested.
7. Lou wished he were in Cadiz.
8. Long live the king!
9. The Togolander was admitted on condition that he study English.
10. Far be it from me to criticize anyone.

DIRECTIONS   Circle the verb that you prefer in each pair, and be prepared to explain your choice. Style may influence the choice in some sentences.

11. The usher suggested that everyone *move/should move* over one seat.
12. The law requires a driver *be/to be* examined periodically.
13. It is imperative that he *catch/catches* the next bus.
14. *Come/Comes* September, we'll be back in school.
15. If she *was/were* here, I could find her.
16. If she *was/were* here, I missed her in the crowd.
17. He decided that if he *was/were* to be on time, he would have to hurry.
18. He suspects that even if he *was/were* on time, he couldn't get on the plane.
19. If I *was/were* Hamlet, I wouldn't trust Claudius either.
20. If I *was/were* Hamlet, who was Horatio?

3.16   Forms of the Modal Auxiliaries   (Ref: CGCE 3.48–55)

DIRECTIONS   The starred expressions are unacceptable; the others are acceptable:

*He mays.	He may.	*He move.	He moves.
*Does he will?	Will he?	*Walks he?	Does he walk?
*He doesn't can.	He can't.	*He climbn't.	He doesn't climb.

In what three ways do **modals** like *may, will,* and *can* differ from other verbs?

1. a. _____

    b. _____

    c. _____

DIRECTIONS   In some meanings, the modals show past time by their past forms (*will/would, can/could, may/might, shall/should*); in other meanings, they show past time by their perfective forms (*will/will have*) or by other verbs (*must/had to*). Supply the appropriate form of each italicized modal for past time.

2. Phil *can* do the backstroke. Last year Phil _____ do the backstroke.

3. My father says I *may* use the car. My father said I _____ use the car yesterday.

4. He *will* not answer. He _____ not answer yesterday.

5. We *must* try harder. We _____ try harder last week.

6. It *may* rain. It _____ rained yesterday.

7. You *can't* be trying. You _____ been trying so far.

8. It *must* be raining. It _____ rained this morning.

9. They *will* finish soon. They _____ finished by now.

10. She *ought to* study. She _____ studied before this.

11. I *shall* do it. I _____ done it by then.

3.17   Uses of the Modal Auxiliaries

(Ref: CGCE 3.48–53)

DIRECTIONS   Fill each blank with a **modal** that will give the sense indicated in parentheses. More than one answer is possible in some sentences.

EXAMPLE   Anyone ____**can**____ make a mistake. (it is possible for anyone to)

1. George _____ tie a square knot. (is able to)

2. Sheila _____ have dessert if she wants it. (is allowed to)

3. A river _____ overflow its banks. (it is theoretically possible for it to)

4. The river _____ have overflowed its banks. (it is possible that it has)

5. Mark _____ swim when he was two. (was able to)

6. _____ we dance? (do you want to?)

7. Theodore _____ study Greek. (has an obligation to)

8. It's too bad that they _____ act like that. (happen to)

9. I _____ be glad if they were to visit us. (my being glad is contingent on their visit)

10. He _____ practice the tuba, in spite of the neighbors. (I insist on it)

11. He _____ practice the tuba, in spite of the neighbors. (he insists on it)

12. It _____ rain this afternoon. (I predict it)

13. The porter _____ carry your bags. (is willing to)

14. He _____ have an omelet for lunch every day. (it was customary for him to)

15. The green stuff _____ be guacamole. (probably is)

16. You _____n't stand on your head. (are not obliged to)

17. You _____n't stand on your head. (are obliged not to)

18. The angles of a triangle _____ total 180°. (it is logically necessary that)

19. The angles of a triangle _____ not exceed 180°. (it is logically necessary that)

● 4.1   Nouns and the Noun Phrase   (Ref: CGCE 4.1, App I.14–17)

DIRECTIONS   Many **nouns** have suffixes that help to identify their part of speech. Write the suffix that ends each noun.

EXAMPLE   gangster   **-ster**

1. puppy _____	14. realism _____	27. infirmity _____
2. siding _____	15. booklet _____	28. communion _____
3. hunter _____	16. nunnery _____	29. withdrawal _____
4. packet _____	17. tendency _____	30. insistence _____
5. cupful _____	18. normalcy _____	31. electorate _____
6. growth _____	19. painting _____	32. discussant _____
7. freedom _____	20. magician _____	33. motherhood _____
8. trainee _____	21. escapist _____	34. suburbanite _____
9. honesty _____	22. hireling _____	35. membership _____
10. jewelry _____	23. goodness _____	36. laundromat _____
11. hostess _____	24. supremacy _____	37. mountaineer _____
12. senator _____	25. orphanage _____	38. kitchenette _____
13. beatnik _____	26. amusement _____	39. authorization _____

DIRECTIONS   A **noun phrase** has a noun or pronoun as its **head word** and may also include **modifiers** of several sorts. Put parentheses around the noun phrases.

EXAMPLE   **(The girl)** told **(Robert)** about **(it)**.

40. The dog buried a bone in our garden.
41. Squirrels hide nuts for the winter.
42. Philip showed us around that factory.
43. He was trying to hide something.
44. Everyone liked both movies.

4.2   Count and Noncount Nouns

(Ref: CGCE 4.2–4)

DIRECTIONS   **Count nouns** can form a plural and can be modified by words like *a,* *an, every, many* (*a bottle, many bottles*). **Noncount nouns** have no plural and can be modified by words like *much* (*much furniture*). Show whether each italicized noun is count (C) or noncount (N) in use by writing the appropriate letter in the parentheses.

EXAMPLE   The *cat* (**C**) likes the *warmth* (**N**) of the *chair* (**C**).

1. Sam ordered a *glass* (   ) of *beer* (   ).
2. Does a German or a Japanese *beer* (   ) have fuller *body* (   )?
3. *Glass* (   ) is a very fragile *material* (   ).
4. Ellen made two *dresses* (   ) from some floursack *material* (   ).
5. *Bravery* (   ) and *discretion* (   ) are compatible *virtues* (   ).
6. A *penny* (   ) for your *thoughts* (   ).
7. *Money* (   ) cannot buy *thought* (   ).
8. Luigi had *pizza* (   ).
9. Luigi ate a *pizza* (   ).
10. *Flatirons* (   ) were made of cast *iron* (   ).

DIRECTIONS   Use each of the following nouns in two sentences, first as a count noun, then as a noncount noun.

11. chicken   (C) _____
              (N) _____
12. television (C) _____
              (N) _____
13. emotion   (C) _____
              (N) _____
14. hair   (C) _____
              (N) _____
15. exercise   (C) _____
              (N) _____

NAME _____ SCORE _____

4.3 Determiners, Predeterminers, Postdeterminers (Ref: CGCE 4.5–15)

DIRECTIONS Determiners are *the, a, an,* and words that can replace them. **Pre-** and **postdeterminers** are closed-system items that come respectively before and after determiners. Circle the determiners, underline the predeterminers once, and underline the postdeterminers twice.

EXAMPLE All (the) other voters have cast (their) ballots.

1. Each woman carried some placards.
2. Neither parent recognized either child.
3. Whose dog is that dachshund?
4. Which car has enough gas?
5. Does any car have much gas?
6. Every other day Hubert goes fishing.
7. They couldn't eat half those fish they caught.
8. All her brothers are here.
9. Both her contact lenses were lost.
10. It made double the work.
11. He made one-third the mistakes I did.
12. We'll take these two magazines.
13. There is no second bell.
14. Let's have a last dance.
15. The next meeting is tomorrow.

DIRECTIONS Arrange each group of words into a coherent noun phrase.

16. a fresh little milk _____
17. days few next sunny the _____
18. a deal extra great of time _____
19. both buildings other tall the two _____
20. answers few last our wrong _____

4.4 Quantifiers

(Ref: CGCE 4.13–15)

DIRECTIONS **Quantifiers** are expressions that specify the number or amount of the following noun, count or noncount. Circle the quantifier that is most appropriate.

1. I'll bet I've got *fewer / less* cavities than you.
2. Wyoming has *fewer / less* population per square mile than Nebraska.
3. Are there *many / much* more students here this year than last?
4. Is there *many / much* more news?
5. All the refrigerator has in it is *a little / several* carrots.
6. Every Chinese meal needs *a little / several* rice along with it.
7. To paint the room would take only *a few / few* hours and *a little / little* effort.
8. You can't help because we have *a few / few* brushes and *a little / little* paint.

DIRECTIONS **Phrasal quantifiers** are word groups ending with *of*. Some phrasal quantifiers allow noncount nouns to be counted. Fill the blanks with appropriate words to make a phrasal quantifier.

9. Waldo's term paper showed _____ of imagination, but it also had _____ of mistakes.
10. Charlotte has two _____ of news for you.
11. My roommate wants to borrow a _____ of paper.
12. To make a sandwich, he puts a _____ of meat between two _____ of bread.
13. For breakfast he had three _____ of coffee and a _____ of porridge.
14. He puts a _____ of salt and several _____ of butter on his soft-boiled eggs.
15. In her bag she carries a _____ of scissors and many _____ of thread.
16. The farm has a hundred _____ of cattle.

4.5   Specific and Generic Reference   (Ref: CGCE 4.16–22)

DIRECTIONS   Some noun phrases have **specific** referents:

   A/The dog is on the porch. (The) dogs are on the porch.

Generic noun phrases refer to a type or class:

   A/The dog is man's best friend. Dogs are man's best friend.

Indicate whether each italicized noun phrase has specific (S) or generic (G) reference by writing the appropriate letter in the parentheses.

EXAMPLE   *Two tigers* (**S**) are sleeping in the cage; *tigers* (**G**) are dangerous.

 1. *The whale* (   ) is *a mammal* (   ).
 2. Yesterday, *the sailor* (   ) spotted *a whale* (   ).
 3. *Some theater-goers* (   ) prefer *comedy* (   ) to *tragedy* (   ).
 4. *This comedy* (   ) will appeal to *theater-goers* (   ).
 5. Only *the brave* (   ) deserve *the fair* (   ).
 6. Only *the brave* (   ) is smoking *his peace pipe* (   ).
 7. *The good* (   ) is what *philosophers* (   ) try to discover.
 8. I know *an Irishman* (   ) who thinks *the Irish* (   ) are peaceful.
 9. Eat *your spinach* (   ) because *spinach* (   ) is good for you.
10. There is *a bird nest* (   ) in *the tree* (   ) over there.

DIRECTIONS   Notice the aspect of the verb in these sentences:

   GENERIC   The tiger is a carnivore. A tiger hunts.

   SPECIFIC   The tiger is being fretful. A tiger is hunting.
             That tiger is fretful. The tigers hunt.

11. Which aspect of the verb can be used with specific reference, but not with generic? _____

4.6   Use of the Articles   (Ref: CGCE 4.17–22)

DIRECTIONS   Fill each blank with the most appropriate of the following **articles:** *the, a, an.* Put an X in any blank where no article seems appropriate. If there is more than one possibility in a blank, be prepared to discuss what, if any, difference of meaning is involved.

1. _____ human body is composed mainly of _____ water.
2. _____ races are not always won by _____ swift.
3. _____ Swiss, _____ Austrians, and _____ Dutch speak _____ Germanic languages.
4. He likes _____ hollandaise sauce on _____ asparagus.
5. Have you ever listened to _____ Japanese music or watched _____ Chinese operas?
6. There is _____ squirrel in _____ next tree, eating _____ nuts; _____ squirrel got _____ nuts from _____ tree in our yard.
7. _____ newspaper today has _____ story about _____ Kentucky Derby.
8. They went down _____ river either by _____ canoe or on _____ raft.
9. Shall we have _____ supper at _____ restaurant or at _____ home?
10. Philbert is studying to be _____ mortician.
11. Prunella wanted to be _____ first woman on _____ moon.
12. They elected him _____ president _____ four times.

DIRECTIONS   Fill each blank with the article that best expresses the meaning in parentheses. Put an X in any blank where no article seems appropriate.

13. _____ bird is eating from our feeder. (specific bird, though I don't expect you to know about it)
14. _____ bird is building a nest. (specific bird that I expect you to know about)
15. _____ birds are related to reptiles. (all members of the class)
16. Would you like to have _____ bird as pet? (some member of the class)
17. _____ woodpecker is insectivorous. (the class as a whole)
18. Eloise wants to be _____ editor. (occupation she aims at)
19. Eloise wants to be _____ editor. (particular job she wants)
20. Eloise wants to be _____ Editor. (title of particular job she wants)

4.7 Proper Names (Ref: CGCE 4.23–30)

DIRECTIONS **Proper names** and some other words are usually capitalized. Circle the words that are usually capitalized.

EXAMPLE The library has paintings of all the presidents since (george) (washington).

1. My grandmother thinks independence day should be the first monday in july.
2. Did you know that grandmother once met president herbert hoover?
3. It is summer in argentina, south of the equator, while it is winter in the northern hemisphere.
4. The golden gate bridge in san francisco is one of the most famous sights west of the rockies.
5. Does the east end at the alleghenies or extend all the way to the mississippi river?

DIRECTIONS Most names are generally used without an article, but some regularly take *the*. Write *the* in the blanks before those names with which it is generally used; put an X in the blanks before names that do not generally take an article.

EXAMPLES __the__ Hague; __X__ Brussels

6. __the__ *Chicago Tribune*
7. _____ *Playboy* unique ?
8. __the__ Metropolitan Museum
9. _____ Madison Square Garden
10. _____ Lake Okeechobee
11. _____ Great Salt Lake
12. __the__ Virgin Islands collective.
13. _____ Staten Island
14. _____ Whitehall
15. __the__ Supreme Court collective.

16. _____ Rice University
17. __the__ University of Michigan
18. __the__ Avenue of the Americas
19. _____ Broadway
20. __the__ Bronx
21. _____ Brooklyn
22. _____ Labor Day
23. __the__ Fourth of July
24. __the__ Prince of Wales
25. _____ Prince Igor

4.8   Number: Subject Concord, Invariable Nouns   (Ref: CGCE 4.31–35)

DIRECTIONS   The number of a noun functioning as subject may be reflected in the form of the verb (**subject concord**). Some nouns, which may be either singular or plural in form, do not have number contrast but are **invariable.** Some take singular verbs, others plural. Circle the form of the verb that is most appropriate to the subject. In some sentences either form is possible; choose the one that seems most natural.

EXAMPLE   Linguistics *is* / are the study of language.

1. The newspaper *is* / *are* full of stories about a new space probe.
2. The stories *has* / *have* been repeated over TV as well.
3. All of the milk *was* / *were* sour.
4. All on the committee *was* / *were* ready to adjourn.
5. The news about the storms *has* / *have* finally reached us.
6. Measles *is* / *are* preventable nowadays.
7. Mathematics *was* / *were* my favorite subject.
8. Dominoes *is* / *are* a very old game.
9. Dominoes *is* / *are* scattered all over the table.
10. The United States *has* / *have* been independent since 1776.
11. The scissors *needs* / *need* to be sharpened.
12. The Middle Ages *was* / *were* full of variety.
13. Campaign headquarters *opens* / *open* next week.
14. The environs of the city *is* / *are* getting crowded.
15. The police *has* / *have* been called.
16. Our thanks *goes* / *go* to an anonymous correspondent.
17. The unschooled *is* / *are* a small minority of the populace.
18. The furniture *was* / *were* all in disorder.
19. The Palisades *is* / *are* along the Hudson River.
20. The waterworks *is* / *are* on the other side of town.

4.9 Noun Plurals

(Ref: CGCE 4.36–57; 3.5)

DIRECTIONS Spell the regular **plural** of the following **singular** nouns, and indicate whether the ending is pronounced /z/, /s/, or /ɪz/ (/əz/).

EXAMPLE hand _____ **hands /z/** _____

1. hat _____
2. dog _____
3. lamp _____
4. toe _____
5. dove _____
6. pass _____
7. pill _____
8. cough _____

9. fox _____
10. load _____
11. church _____
12. ridge _____
13. cook _____
14. buzz _____
15. flush _____
16. depth _____

DIRECTIONS Some of the following nouns have plurals that are irregular; others are regular. Spell the plural of each.

17. tray _____
18. fly _____
19. 98 _____
20. VIP _____
21. hero _____
22. piano _____
23. knife _____
24. safe _____
25. goose _____
26. woman _____
27. child _____
28. salmon _____
29. series _____

30. larva _____
31. alumnus _____
32. index _____
33. crisis _____
34. chassis _____
35. tableau _____
36. libretto _____
37. kibbutz _____
38. phenomenon _____
39. bacterium _____
40. girl friend _____
41. brother-in-law _____
42. gentleman scholar _____

4.10   Gender

(Ref: CGCE 4.58–65)

DIRECTIONS   Some nouns have separate forms to denote males and females. What are the distinctively **feminine** forms that correspond to these **masculine** nouns?

1. nephew   _____
2. bridegroom _____
3. drum major _____
4. actor   _____
5. hero   _____
6. boy friend _____

7. lion   _____
8. gander   _____
9. bull   _____
10. peacock _____
11. he-goat _____
12. stallion _____

DIRECTIONS   The **gender** of a noun is indicated by the pronouns that substitute for it. Write the appropriate pronoun (*who, which; he, she, it, they*) for the italicized noun. If more than one is possible, write all.

13. This is our *hostess*, _____ wants to know whether _____ can help.

14. A *monk*, _____ gets a tonsure when _____ professes, wears a cap.

15. My only *cousin*, _____ lives in Nova Scotia, visits us when _____ can.

16. This *infant*, _____ is an orphan, acts as though _____ is hungry.

17. The senior *class*, _____ had a meeting, decided _____ would hold a dance.

18. The white *stallion*, _____ is in the stable, is saddled, so _____ can be raced.

19. The old *hen*, _____ is a Rhode Island Red, is under the porch, where _____ likes to nest.

20. That *robin*, _____ built a nest in the tree, has young birds _____ feeds.

21. Have you seen their *sloop*, _____ is in the dock? Isn't _____ a beauty?

22. They gave us a *television*, _____ is what we wanted, but _____ is broken.

23. The green *frog*, _____ the cat was chasing, looks as if _____ is stunned.

24. Tell the next *person* _____ calls that _____ can make an appointment.

4.11 Form and Meaning of the Genitive   (Ref: CGCE 4.66–70)

DIRECTIONS In addition to the **common case** (*boy*), nouns have also a **genitive case,** often an inflected **'s-genitive** (*boy's*); sometimes a prepositional phrase, the *of-genitive* (*of the boy*), is used instead. Write the *'s*-genitive of each of the following.

1. girl _____
2. girls _____
3. prince _____
4. princes _____
5. woman _____
6. women _____
7. jury _____
8. juries _____

9. Jones _____
10. the Joneses _____
11. Socrates _____
12. (for) goodness (sake) _____
13. Prince of Sikkim _____
14. Princes of Sikkim _____
15. the man from Rome _____
16. a man I know _____

DIRECTIONS The meaning of a genitive can be shown by paraphrasing it as a sentence or phrase: *my son's wife = My son has a wife.* Paraphrase each of the following genitives so as to show the meaning of the construction.

17. the nurse's new uniform _____
18. the committee's decision _____
19. the prisoner's release _____
20. Shakespeare's last play _____
21. a children's zoo _____
22. the length of the journey _____
23. the state of Montana _____
24. the man's weight _____
25. an eclipse of the moon _____
26. Canada's great mountains _____
27. the flight of the bird _____

4.12 Uses of the Genitive (Ref: CGCE 4.69–77)

DIRECTIONS Combine each pair of sentences by rephrasing the first as either an *'s*-genitive, an *of*-genitive, or a double genitive (as in *a play of Shaw's,* in which *of Shaw's* combines the *of*- and *'s*-genitives). There is often more than one possibility.

EXAMPLE Geraldine has a neighbor. The neighbor is growing periwinkles.

Geraldine's neighbor is growing periwinkles.

1. The plane departed. That event was late.

2. The lion was captured. The event was exciting.

3. The man baked a cake. The cake won first prize.

4. The store is for men. The store is having a sale.

5. The city is Chicago. The city is on Lake Michigan.

6. The team has a coach. The coach called an extra practice.

7. The vacation lasted a week. He was given a vacation.

8. The hand is part of the clock. The hand is on twelve.

9. The man across the street has a dog. The dog bit me.

10. Jim took a test. Our test was harder than that was.

11. Plato had students. Aristotle was such a student.

12. The doctor has an office. I'll meet you there.

4.13   Central Pronouns   (Ref: CGCE 4.78–87)

DIRECTIONS   There are many kinds of **pronouns**. The **central** pronouns involve a choice among forms, including those for **case** (**subjective** and **objective**), **person**, **gender**, and **number**. Fill the blank with an appropriate form of a central pronoun to refer to the italicized expression. Be prepared to describe what difference in effect is created by various choices.

1. _____He_____ and ____I____ are going to paint the house together.   (*George* and *the speaker*)

2. There may be only ____us____ left in the building.   (*the speaker and someone else*)

3. Blessed be _____him_____ that blesses others.   (*a person*)

4. —Is *George* there? —That is ____him____.

5. *Herman* did it, and it is _____ _____ self who is to blame.

6. The last person I expect to see on a roller coaster is ____her____. (*Mary*)

7. Angela studied longer than ____they____ did.   (*Sue and Mary*)

8. Angela studied longer than ____they____ ~~them~~ (*Sue and Mary*)

9. The old lady was kind to ____my____ brother and ____me____. (I ?) (*the speaker*)

10. The judges want both you and ____her____ to perform again.   (*Mary*)

11. *We* watched the excitement all around ____us____.

12. *John and George* each pulled _____ coats closer around

   _____.

13. *I'm* going to get ____me____ some supper and then go to bed.

14. *George* cut _____ while he was shaving.

15. *Laura* wrote a letter to the congressman _____.

16. Laura wrote a letter to the *congressman* _____.

17. *All the people* in our apartment house know _____.

18. *Phil and Lou* are going to help _____. (Phil will help Lou and vice versa)

19. *A person* needs to know what to do if _____ finds _____ in an emergency.

20. —You had a call this afternoon. —What did ____he, she____ want? (*the caller*)
   ____they____

4.14   Relatives, Interrogatives, Demonstratives   (Ref: CGCE 4.88–90)

DIRECTIONS   The **relative** and **interrogative** pronouns involve choices of several kinds. Fill the blank with the form that seems most appropriate.

1. My mother, _____ was once a chorus girl, has a trunkful of momentos.
2. Angela, to _____ the novel is dedicated, is a mystery woman.
3. _____ did you want to talk to?
4. _____ do you suppose that is, wearing a veil?
5. They used to live in Miami, _____ was a small town in those days.
6. Have you ever lived in a town _____ had only one store in it?
7. Is the girl _____ Jerome wants to marry an etymologist?
8. _____ of those subjects are you majoring in?
9. _____ in all the world would you most like to learn?
10. Seth is the one _____ grandmother was an ecdysiast.
11. You can read anything you want and think _____ you please.
12. They are giving peacock feathers to _____ wants them.
13. _____ you say, it wasn't Sheila.
14. Albert intends to read _____ book is shorter.

DIRECTIONS   The **demonstrative** pronouns and determiners are *this/these* and *that/those*. Fill each blank with the most appropriate form.

15. _____ pebbles in my hand are quite different from _____ over there in the creek.
16. _____ is what he must do: listen and not talk.
17. Early to bed and early to rise—_____ is what the rime says to do.
18. Stop me if you've heard _____ story.
19. _____ was a long introduction the M.C. gave the speaker.
20. _____ who are able ought to volunteer.
21. Carmichael likes to do _____ which is difficult.

4.15   Universal Pronouns   (Ref: CGCE 4.91)

DIRECTIONS   **Universal** pronouns and determiners are *all, both, each, every, everybody, everyone, everything*. Fill each blank with the form that is most appropriate.

1. _____ clouds are made of water vapor.

2. _____ cloud is one of ten basic types.

3. _____ cloud is nevertheless different from _____ others.

4. The birds have _____ gone south for the winter.

5. We can _____ go to a different movie.

6. _____ has to get ready for the holiday.

7. The twins are _____ visiting their grandmother.

8. You'll find _____ you need in the trunk.

9. _____ in her sorority likes _____ one of the other members.

DIRECTIONS   Most universal pronouns can be referred to by personal and possessive pronouns that are either singular or plural. Fill each blank with the personal or possessive pronoun that is most appropriate for referring to the universal pronoun in the sentence.

10. Everybody did what _____ liked best.

11. Everyone started the test late, but _____ will finish on time.

12. If everybody is happy, why should _____ complain.

13. When girl scouts camp out, each has to put up _____ own tent.

14. Each of them wanted to have _____ own way.

15. When a husband and wife travel together, each will receive a reduction on _____ ticket.

16. All of them put on _____ coats and left.

17. All of the bread has lost _____ freshness.

18. Everything went wrong this morning, but we got _____ all fixed.

4.16 Partitive Pronouns; General Quantifiers (Ref: CGCE 4.92–95)

DIRECTIONS Fill each blank with the most appropriate **partitive** pronoun: *any, some* (*-one, -body, -thing*); *none, nobody, no one, nothing; neither, either.*

1. Matilda found _____ of the missing coins, but Al didn't find

    _____ .

2. The coffee is stronger than you like it. Do you want _____?

3. There's plenty of fresh coffee. Wouldn't you like _____?

4. Huxley did more to popularize the theory of evolution than _____ else.

5. There must be _____ wrong with the car again.

6. Some particles travel very rapidly, but _____ of them exceed the speed of light, because _____ is able to travel faster than that.

7. The clock is broken, so _____ knows what time it is.

8. The alligator might have caught _____ of Simon's legs, but luckily it got _____ of them.

DIRECTIONS Rewrite the following sentence to make it negative. There are several ways it can be negated.

9. Bertram met someone who told him something about Afghanistan.

    _____

DIRECTIONS Circle the most appropriate **general quantifier,** and be prepared to explain why you think it is best.

10. Although the polls closed at six, *few / little* of the vote is in because *few / little* of the votes have been counted yet.

11. Over 60,000 persons are registered to vote, but considerably *fewer / less* are eligible for today's election.

12. *Many / Much* of the jury wanted to convict the defendant.

13. The corn looks fresh, but we are afraid *many / much* of it won't be.

14. Hernando's delicatessen has *enough / several* waiters, but needs more.

15. Hernando has *enough / several* business to open another store.

4.17   One and Numerals

(Ref: CGCE 4.96–97)

DIRECTIONS   The word *one* has **numerical** (N), **replacing** (R), and **indefinite** (I) uses. Identify the use of each italicized *one* by writing the appropriate letter in the parentheses.

1. Four almanacs are more than I want—I need only *one* (   ).

2. Zoe likes the old Bergman films, but I prefer the newer *ones* (   ).

3. *One* (   ) of the tires is flat, but the other is all right.

4. *One* (   ) hopes it will be a short, cool summer.

5. I'm going to the deli for a sandwich. Can I bring you *one* (   )?

6. He is *one* (   ) of those who always expect the worst.

DIRECTIONS   Indefinite *one* tends to be formal in its use. Rephrase each sentence to replace indefinite *one* with some less formal expression.

7. If one has a cold, one should drink liquids and rest.

   _____

8. One regrets seeing open fields made into parking lots.

   _____

9. One should remember how insignificant one really is.

   _____

10. That is not the way one says it in Canada.

   _____

DIRECTIONS   Fill the blanks with appropriate words for **numerals.**

11. Two plus two is _____. Three minus three is _____.

12. A quartet consists of _____ persons. An empty room has _____ persons in it.

13. They each had five pencils. She gave one away, so now has _____. He gave all of his away, so now has _____.

Note how terms for *0* differ from terms for other numbers.

4.18   Pronouns

(Ref: CGCE 4.78–97)

DIRECTIONS   **Central** pronouns are **personal** (Per), **reflexive** (Ref), **reciprocal** (Rec), and **possessive** (Pos). Identify the kind of each italicized central pronoun by writing the appropriate symbol in the parentheses.

1. Give *yourself* (   ) a chance to learn French.

2. *You* (   ) and *I* (   ) have to do it *ourselves* (   ).

3. John wants Paul to give *him* (   ) a haircut and to get one *himself* (   ).

4. Amy has finished *her* (   ) shopping; *it* (   ) exhausted *her* (   ).

5. *My* (   ) parents have persuaded *each other* (   ) not to exchange presents.

6. *His* (   ) relatives see *one another* (   ) on holidays and on *their* (   ) vacations.

7. *They* (   ) didn't like *one another's* (   ) answers, or *mine* (   ), or *hers* (   ).

DIRECTIONS   By writing the appropriate abbreviation in parentheses, indicate whether the italicized pronouns are **central** (C), **relative** (R), **interrogative** (I), **demonstrative** (D), **universal** (U), **partitive** (P), or **quantifying** (Q).

8. James told *us* (   ) all about *himself* (   ).

9. Lola and Nina lent *their* (   ) clothes to *each other* (   ).

10. *Who* (   ) picked up the book *that* (   ) was here?

11. *Everyone* (   ) at the barbecue had *some* (   ) of the spareribs.

12. As Marilyn poured the coffee, *he* (   ) said, "*That* (   ) is *enough* (   )."

13. *Many* (   ) of the bees did not sting *anyone* (   ).

14. *Which* (   ) of the umbrellas is *yours* (   )?

15. *This* (   ) will appeal to *both* (   ) of the twins.

16. General Bullwinkle, *who* (   ) works at the Pentagon, promoted *them* (   ).

17. Calm *yourselves* (   ), and pay attention to *one another* (   ).

18. *Each* (   ) of the cabs seats *more* (   ) than *six* (   ).

● 5.1 Characteristics of the Adjective (Ref: CGCE 5.1–2, App I.19–21)

DIRECTIONS Some **adjectives** have suffixes that help to identify their part of speech. Write the suffix that ends each adjective.

EXAMPLE   helpful   **-ful**

1. topmost _____
2. sandy _____
3. metallic _____
4. wooden _____
5. horned _____
6. famous _____
7. active _____

8. likeable _____
9. fishlike _____
10. fearless _____
11. national _____
12. womanly _____
13. sheepish _____
14. infantile _____

15. Jeffersonian _____
16. evolutionary _____
17. contradictory _____
18. compassionate _____
19. picturesque _____
20. troublesome _____
21. trustworthy _____

DIRECTIONS Most adjectives have **comparative** and **superlative** forms, either with suffixes (*great, greater, greatest*) or with modifiers (*beautiful, more beautiful, most beautiful*). Write *Aj* before the words that can be compared in either of those ways and *X* before the others.

22. _____ tall
23. _____ deep
24. _____ talk
25. _____ foot

26. _____ fast
27. _____ although
28. _____ statue
29. _____ neat

30. _____ statuesque
31. _____ possible
32. _____ rapid
33. _____ wakeful

DIRECTIONS Most adjectives can be modified by the **intensifier** *very*. Insert *very* before each adjective.

EXAMPLE   The performance by the **very** beautiful actress was **very** fine.

34. A circus acrobat was amusing the little children.
35. The skillful acrobat was amusing to the children.
36. The witness was confused by the rapid questions.
37. The answers were confused and uncertain.
38. The two small sports cars were parked in the crowded lot.

5.2   Adjective Phrases

DIRECTIONS   An **adjective phrase** consists of an adjective as **head,** which may be **modified** by other words:

happy	happy that he is here
quite happy	as happy as can be
so very happy	much happier
happy enough	happier than George
happy about it	happier than he used to be
happy to see you	happiest of all

Underline each adjective phrase.

1. The skier was altogether exhausted.

2. The snow was blindingly white.

3. The squirrels were happy to see William.

4. Don't be quite so curious.

5. She was amazed at his audacity.

6. The tea is hotter than it was yesterday.

DIRECTIONS   Add **modifiers** to each italicized adjective, and write the resulting adjective phrase in the blank.

EXAMPLE   Phil was *anxious.*   __**extremely anxious for us to leave**__

7. His hair is *short.*   _____

8. The man is *old.*   _____

9. The questions were *difficult.* _____

10. Angela was *glad.*   _____

11. The knife will be *useful.*   _____

12. Samson was *angrier.*   _____

13. The umpire was *certain.*   _____

14. His answer was *different.*   _____

15. The bell was *louder.*   _____

16. They were *easiest.*   _____

5.3 Syntactic Functions of Adjectives (1)   (Ref: CGCE 5.3–11)

DIRECTIONS   Adjective phrases have the following syntactic functions:

(A)   **Attributive:** the *beautiful* painting
(Cs)   **Subject complement:** Your daughter is *pretty.*
(Co)   **Object complement:** He made his wife *happy.*
(P)   **Postpositive:** the people *involved*
(AP)   **Attributive with postposed complementation:** the *best* nut *to eat*
(N)   **Head of a noun phrase:** the *extremely old* (need Medicare.)
(VC)   **Verbless clause:** *Very nervous,* the man opened the letter.
(ES)   **Exclamatory sentence:** *How good of you!*

In each sentence, underline the adjective phrase and indicate its function by writing the appropriate letters in the blank.

EXAMPLE   An <u>unusually honest</u> man returned my wallet.   __A__

1. He found a counterfeit banknote.   _____

2. An antique map was hanging on the wall.   _____

3. He suggested the obvious.   _____

4. How nice for her!   _____

5. The bus was completely full.   _____

6. A strange thing was happening.   _____

7. Uncertain about driving, they decided to take the bus.   _____

8. Johnson is taller than I am.   _____

9. Louis left his room messy.   _____

10. The race is not always to the swift.   _____

11. You can return these bottles, when empty.   _____

12. That is a difficult question to answer.   _____

13. We found the movie very dull.   _____

14. Bread fresh from the oven is what he likes.   _____

15. The document has to be certified by a notary public.   _____

16. Everyone is ready to go.   _____

5.4 Syntactic Functions of Adjectives (2) (Ref: CGCE 5.3—11)

DIRECTIONS Combine the sentences in each pair by inserting the second into the first as an adjective phrase. Be prepared to identify the syntactic function of each phrase.

EXAMPLE He framed the painting. The painting was beautiful.

He framed the beautiful painting.

1. A doctor conducted the examination. He was very skeptical.

2. They painted their bedroom. As a result, the bedroom was light blue.

3. Those persons should have some other pet. They are allergic to cats.

4. The Philberts were guests. They were the last to arrive.

5. The instructor assigned a book. It was too long to read in a week.

6. The acrobats bounded onto the stage. They were ready to perform.

7. The material can be stretched. That is, while it is wet.

8. The driver crossed the finish line. He was tired but happy.

9. They found the children. The children were asleep.

10. We arrived at the castle one night. The night was dark and stormy.

5.5   Syntactic Subclassification of Adjectives   (Ref: CGCE 5.12–18)

DIRECTIONS   Some adjectives are only **attributive** (that is, used before nouns): *an utter fool,* not **the fool is utter.* Others are only **predicative** (that is, used after verbs like *be*): *the woman is loath to admit it,* not **a loath woman.* Most adjectives are **central** (that is, either attributive or predicative): *a hungry man* or *the man is hungry.* Write the appropriate letter after each expression to indicate whether the adjective in it is attributive only (A), predicative only (P), or central (C).

1. the main problem _____
2. the great pleasure _____
3. the sheer pleasure _____
4. a medical student _____
5. a medical problem _____
6. The boy is healthy. _____
7. The patient got well. _____
8. The man is alone. _____
9. his little (younger) sister _____
10. his little (small) car _____
11. a long-time acquaintance _____
12. Her brother was aware of it. _____
13. A duck is fond of water. _____
14. The mouse was afraid. _____
15. The bird was fearful. _____
16. The play is tragic. _____

DIRECTIONS   Rephrase each sentence to turn part of it into an attributive adjective.

EXAMPLE   The man who is tall is the coach.
        The tall man is the coach.

17. She cooked a sauce that was very spicy.

_____

18. The program that is funniest is on next.

_____

19. That comedian has a style that is urbane.

_____

20. An answer that is quiet will turn aside wrath.

_____

21. The acrobat did a somersault that was perfect.

_____

5.6 Semantic Subclassification of Adjectives   (Ref: CGCE 5.19–20)

DIRECTIONS **Dynamic** adjectives can be used after a progressive form of *be* and in commands: *He is being careful. Be careful.* **Stative** adjectives cannot: **He is being tall. *Be tall.* Indicate whether each adjective is dynamic (D) or stative (S) by writing the appropriate letter in the blank.

1. good _____   5. active _____   9. nuclear _____

2. thin _____   6. asleep _____   10. serious _____

3. round _____   7. woolen _____   11. mountainous _____

4. quiet _____   8. hopeful _____   12. enthusiastic _____

DIRECTIONS **Gradable** adjectives can be freely compared and intensified: *taller, tallest, very tall; more beautiful, most beautiful.* **Nongradable** adjectives cannot: **more atomic, *most atomic, *very atomic.* Indicate whether each adjective is gradable (G) or nongradable (N) by writing the appropriate letter in the blank.

13. nice _____   17. oaken _____   21. anxious _____

14. thin _____   18. entire _____   22. nuclear _____

15. main _____   19. Ohioan _____   23. optical _____

16. warm _____   20. ancient _____   24. inquisitive _____

DIRECTIONS **Inherent** adjectives can be paraphrased as follows: *a new car = It is a new thing and it is a car* (not **It is new as a car*). **Noninherent** adjectives can be paraphrased as follows: *a new friend = He is new as a friend* (not **He is a new person and he is a friend*). The same adjective can be inherent or noninherent, depending on the noun it is used with. Identify the adjectives as inherent (I) or noninherent (N) by writing the appropriate letter in the blank.

25. an accomplished actress _____   31. an Italian actress _____

26. a blue dress _____   32. a poor choice _____

27. a big circle _____   33. a poor person _____

28. a big mistake _____   34. a possible answer _____

29. an eager student _____   35. a thin pianist _____

30. a good pianist _____   36. a wooden building _____

5.7 Characteristics of the Adverb   (Ref: CGCE 5.21, App I.22)

DIRECTIONS   Some **adverbs** have suffixes or suffixlike endings that help to identify their part of speech. Write the ending of each adverb.

1. nearly	_____	6. crossways	_____
2. onward	_____	7. nationwide	_____
3. likewise	_____	8. straightway	_____
4. sidelong	_____	9. crab-fashion	_____
5. backwards	_____	10. French-style	_____

DIRECTIONS   The most common ending for adverbs is the *-ly* that is added to adjectives to make a process adverb (*happily* 'in a happy manner'). There is, however, also an adjective-forming *-ly* ending that is added to nouns (*kingly* 'characteristic of a king') or to a few adjectives (*cleanly* 'tending to be clean'). Indicate whether each of the following words is an adverb (Av) or an adjective (Aj) by writing the appropriate abbreviation in the blank.

11. friendly	_____	19. lively	_____	27. humbly	_____
12. royally	_____	20. lovely	_____	28. lowly	_____
13. expertly	_____	21. nicely	_____	29. fatherly	_____
14. scholarly	_____	22. beautifully	_____	30. quickly	_____
15. learnedly	_____	23. deadly	_____	31. neighborly	_____
16. cowardly	_____	24. mortally	_____	32. repeatedly	_____
17. fearfully	_____	25. shapely	_____	33. worldly	_____
18. manly	_____	26. queenly	_____	34. slowly	_____

DIRECTIONS   Some adverbs have no distinctive ending, but can be recognized by their functioning either as **adverbials** (as in *He did it_____*) or as **modifiers** of adjectives or other adverbs (as in *He is _____ good*). List several endingless adverbs that function in those ways.

35. ADVERBIAL _____

36. MODIFIER _____

5.8   Adverb Phrases   (Ref: CGCE 5.21)

DIRECTIONS   An adverb functions as the **head** of an **adverb phrase,** which may also include **modifiers.** Underline each adverb phrase, and circle the head word.

EXAMPLE   She is more (easily) intelligible.

1. He talks too loudly.
2. A salesman must treat customers more politely.
3. We will leave pretty soon.
4. I left my notebook right here.
5. She discovered diamonds are so terribly expensive.
6. They left sort of quickly.
7. He talked very sincerely.
8. He had a much too eager smile.
9. I'll come right along.
10. She was rather insistently demanding attention.
11. Just then an explosion shook the building.
12. She skis well enough for the winter Olympics.

DIRECTIONS   The modifier in an adverb phrase may itself be an adverb phrase. Thus in the adverb phrase *far more easily,* the head is *easily* and the modifier is *far more,* an adverb phrase with the head *more* and the modifier *far.* Underline the head of the whole phrase twice and the head of the modifying phrase once.

EXAMPLE   not so eagerly

13. altogether too soon
14. so very ominously
15. much more stealthily
16. just about here
17. somewhat less helpfully
18. rather more honestly
19. quite as promptly
20. almost exactly then

5.9   Adverbs as Adverbials   (Ref: CGCE 5.22)

DIRECTIONS   Combine the sentences in each pair by inserting the meaning of the second into the first as an **adverbial.**

EXAMPLE   They are waiting. They are outside.

They are waiting outside. _____

1. The traffic moved down the road. The movement was slow.

   _____

2. The boys were playing baseball. The game was nearby.

   _____

3. Albert wrote to his senator. The writing was recent.

   _____

4. England was invaded by the Scandinavians. It happened long ago.

   _____

5. The library is closed. That is obvious.

   _____

6. McGoo will run for mayor. That is positive.

   _____

7. He has moved to New York. He was happy about it.

   _____

8. He has moved to New York. I am happy about it.

   _____

DIRECTIONS   Fill the blank in the second clause with an adverb that helps to connect the two clauses.

9. Mr. Blandings made a scarecrow; the birds _____ ate his corn.

10. The little boy bit the dentist's finger. The dentist finished cleaning his teeth _____.

11. The water pipes froze, and _____ we had to drink soda.

12. If you can ride a bicycle, you can learn to ride a unicycle _____.

13. First the dog chased the cat up a tree, but _____ he trotted off.

5.10   Adverbs as Modifiers or Complements   (Ref: CGCE 5.23–30)

DIRECTIONS   Fill each blank with an adverb that functions as a **modifier**. Circle the word or phrase that is modified.

EXAMPLE   The race left Throckmorton **completely** (exhausted).

1. That is _____ hot coffee.
2. The logic of his argument was _____ convincing.
3. The light is not bright _____ to read by.
4. It is _____ possible for man to live in space.
5. He opened the door _____ cautiously.
6. Everyone believed her because she seemed _____ very sure of herself.
7. He walked _____ through the puddle.
8. The visitors ate _____ all the popcorn.
9. We have _____ any of the popcorn left.
10. It was _____ a problem.
11. _____ a busy day this has been!
12. _____ fast can a car go on this road?
13. It was the room _____ that they rented.
14. The journey to Europe was fine, but the trip _____ was rough.

DIRECTIONS   An adverb may also be the **complement of a preposition,** a function usually filled by nouns. Fill each blank with an adverb.

EXAMPLE   He should have been here by_____**now.**_____

15. I haven't seen a movie like that since _____.
16. We'll be glad to wait in _____.
17. He plans to start studying after _____.
18. She brought the coins from _____.

5.11   Functions of the Adverb   (Ref: CGCE 5.21–30)

DIRECTIONS   An adverb or adverb phrase can function as a major sentence element, the **adverbial** (A); as a **modifier** (M), especially of adjectives and adverbs, but also of prepositional phrases, determiners, and noun phrases; and occasionally as the **complement** (C) of a preposition. Indicate the function of each italicized adverb by writing the appropriate letter in parentheses.

EXAMPLES   *Yesterday* (**A**) we spotted a *very* (**M**) energetic bird.

It has been building a nest *industriously* (**A**) since *then* (**C**).

1. Thompson is *rather* (   ) suspicious of anyone who talks *oddly* (   ).
2. *Quite* (   ) a few people think the way Thompson talks is *decidedly* (   ) odd.
3. Until *recently* (   ), Thompson lived *alone* (   ) and *seldom* (   ) traveled.
4. *Luckily* (   ), the rain has been *fairly* (   ) light.
5. Biologists *recently* (   ) made a *medically* (   ) useful discovery.
6. They made the announcement *somewhat* (   ) *reluctantly* (   ).
7. *Furthermore* (   ), airplanes fly *just* (   ) over our house.
8. Walt sat *there* (   ) for *almost* (   ) an hour.
9. He saved *over* (   ) a dozen doughnuts for *later* (   ).
10. Before *now* (   ), *hardly* (   ) anyone studied Tibetan.

DIRECTIONS   To these sentences add adverbs with the functions indicated in parentheses.

<pre>
            Finally   reasonably
EXAMPLE   Mrs. Kapotnik was content. (adverbial, modifier of adjective)
            ^   ^
</pre>

11. Hermione has been singing Wagner ever since. (adverbial, complement)

12. A large dog stood menacingly in the door. (modifiers of adjective and adverb)

13. No one lives near. (modifier of pronoun, complement)

14. He is too tall. (adverbial, modifier of adverb)

79

5.12   Comparison and Gradability   (Ref: CGCE 5.31, 33, 35–38)

DIRECTIONS   Write the **comparative** and **superlative** forms of these adjectives and adverbs. Some are formed with -er and -est, others with *more* and *most*.

EXAMPLES   young   **younger, youngest**   easily   **more easily, most easily**

1. far	_____	12. badly	_____
2. fat	_____	13. early	_____
3. dry	_____	14. kingly	_____
4. tall	_____	15. polite	_____
5. good	_____	16. narrow	_____
6. much	_____	17. tenable	_____
7. near	_____	18. detailed	_____
8. late	_____	19. wholesome	_____
9. gray	_____	20. beautiful	_____
10. able	_____	21. convincing	_____
11. comic	_____	22. independent	_____

DIRECTIONS   **Gradable** adjectives and adverbs can be modified by words like *very* and can be compared. **Nongradable** adjectives and adverbs usually cannot, although they can be modified by qualifying words like *definitely*. When a normally nongradable word is compared or modified by *very*, it develops a somewhat different meaning. Indicate whether each of the following is usually gradable (G) or nongradable (N) by writing the appropriate letter in the blank. Some of the words have been the subject of a good deal of argument. Be prepared to discuss why there has been disagreement.

23. now ___	26. atomic ___	29. perfect ___	32. British ___
24. total ___	27. frozen ___	30. simple ___	33. electric ___
25. alive ___	28. square ___	31. quickly ___	34. potential ___

5.13 Basis of Comparison

(Ref: CGCE 5.32)

DIRECTIONS Combine the sentences in each pair to make the **basis of comparison** explicit in the second sentence.

EXAMPLE Bob is stupid. John is more stupid.

John is more stupid than Bob.

1. Waldo is curious about it. Fred is more curious about it.

_____

2. Ella's brother is impatient. Ella is less impatient.

_____

3. Philbert is nervous. Gary is just as nervous.

_____

4. The Smiths left early. The Joneses left earlier.

_____

5. There are two sleepy children. The little one is the sleepier.

_____

6. These are some dogs. Rover is the fiercest.

_____

DIRECTIONS Circle the form of the pronoun that seems best.

7. Marcia is a good deal quieter than _he_ / _him_.
8. Tilly can read much faster than _he_ / _him_.
9. Black looks better on Mary than _he_ / _him_.
10. Mary was engaged to George longer than _he_ / _him_.
11. Nathan is as tall as _she_ / _her_.
12. Her father spanked her brother as often as _she_ / _her_.

One way to avoid the problem of pronoun form is to expand the postmodifier by adding an auxiliary verb, another pronoun, or a preposition. Orally rephrase the sentences above, with such additions.

5.14 Markedness and Modification   (Ref: CGCE 5.34, 39)

DIRECTIONS Some adjectives and adverbs come in pairs, of which one member, the **unmarked term** (in contrast to the other, the **marked term**), is used regularly in *How-*questions and often to state measurements. Thus we say, *How old is he?* and *He is two years old* without implying that the subject is old. But asking *How young is he?* assumes the subject to be young. Therefore, *old* is the unmarked and *young* the marked member of the pair. In the following pairs, circle the unmarked terms.

1. far / near
2. bad / good
3. short / tall
4. heavy / light

5. flexible / rigid
6. narrow / wide
7. deep / shallow
8. regular / irregular

9. thick / thin
10. loose / tight
11. long / short
12. hard / soft

DIRECTIONS Comparatives and superlatives can be modified just like other adjectives and adverbs. Arrange the words in each group in an appropriate order to make an adjective or adverb phrase.

EXAMPLE carefully less much so very **so very much less carefully**

13. much nicer so very   _____
14. all more readily the   _____
15. a deal faster good   _____
16. a accurately less lot   _____
17. likely more much so   _____
18. a bit farther little   _____
19. by darkest far the   _____
20. interesting less rather   _____
21. more openly somewhat _____
22. most popular the very   _____

5.15   Adjectives and Adverbs   (Ref: CGCE 5.40–41)

DIRECTIONS   Rephrase each sentence so that the italicized adjective is made into an adverb. Make whatever other changes are needed.

EXAMPLE   He liked Mary to a *considerable* extent.

He liked Mary considerably. _____

1. The man in the raincoat is behaving in a *suspicious* manner.

   _____

2. Eloise is afraid of airplanes to a *great* degree.

   _____

3. Puddinhead is immature from an *intellectual* viewpoint.

   _____

4. He has a *firm* belief in free speech.

   _____

5. Floyd ate in a *greedy* way.

   _____

6. Philippa's speech is *clear*.

   _____

7. Olga is a *professional* bridge player.

   _____

8. Herman has a *genuine* interest in diamond-cutting.

   _____

9. Rain was the *chief* cause.

   _____

10. The cook is a *real* master chef.

    _____

11. They made a *recent* move to Chicago.

    _____

5.16 Adjectives, Adverbs, and Nouns (Ref: CGCE 5.42–45)

DIRECTIONS Indicate whether the italicized words are adjectives (Aj) or adverbs (Av) by writing the appropriate symbol in the blanks.

1. The forest was *ablaze*. _____

2. The captain is *aboard*. _____

3. He came *along*. _____

4. He acted *aloof*. _____

5. The baby is *asleep*. _____

6. The neighbors are *away*. _____

7. They had a *long* wait for news. _____

8. They have *long* waited for news. _____

9. They went on an *earlier* trip. _____

10. They went on a trip *earlier*. _____

11. The weather is *daily* getting worse. _____

12. The *daily* weather report is encouraging. _____

13. She had done *hard* work. _____

14. She has worked *hard*. _____

DIRECTIONS Indicate whether the italicized words are adjectives (Aj) or nouns (N) by writing the appropriate symbol in the blanks.

15. She wore a *yellow* dress. _____

16. *Yellow* is a cheerful color. _____

17. He is driving a *convertible*. _____

18. The car is *convertible*. _____

19. They made a *wood* fire. _____

20. They made a *wooden* fence. _____

21. The table has a *false* top. _____

22. The table has a *marble* top. _____

23. The belt is made of *elastic*. _____

24. It is a very *elastic* belt. _____

5.17 Adjectives, Adverbs, and Other Word Classes

(Ref: CGCE 5.46–49)

DIRECTIONS   Indicate whether the italicized words are adjectives (Aj) or participles (P) by writing the appropriate symbol in the blanks.

1. The peasants were *revolting* against their rulers.   _____

2. The peasants were *revolting* to their rulers.   _____

3. The man has been *drunk*.   _____

4. The milk has been *drunk*.   _____

5. His talk is *amusing* to us.   _____

6. His talk is *amusing* us.   _____

7. She was *surprised* at it.   _____

8. She was *surprised* by it.   _____

9. He was *subdued* by the police.   _____

10. He was *subdued* in manner.   _____

DIRECTIONS   For each blank, supply an appropriate adverb that will help to connect the two clauses.

11. The microphone broke, and _____ the speaker had to talk louder.

12. The medicine man did a rain dance, but _____ the drought continued.

13. The garden needs to be fenced, or _____ the rabbits will get in.

14. There is no supply of oil, nor is there of gas _____.

15. The meeting will be outdoors, for _____ everyone can attend.

DIRECTIONS   Supply an appropriate **reaction signal** (like *yes* or *no*) or **initiator** (like *well* or *say*) for each blank.

16. _____, have you seen what's happening in the quad?

17. _____, I've heard about it.

18. _____, you should find out all about it.

19. _____, why should I?

20. _____, if you don't know, I can't tell you.

• 6.1   Prepositional Phrases

(Ref: CGCE 6.1–2, 4)

DIRECTIONS   Put parentheses around each **prepositional phrase.**

EXAMPLE   He was surprised (at her remark.)

1. She drove from her house to her office in ten minutes.
2. Henry lived in Chicago for a long while.
3. The company gave a dinner for Henry on his retirement.
4. Without blinking an eye, Alice shot at the rattlesnake.
5. Phil thought about what he had seen, and then he wrote a description of it.
6. The janitor waited for them to leave before locking the door.
7. Outside the auditorium we listened to their singing.
8. Near the alley, some boys in tennis shoes were pitching pennies.

DIRECTIONS   **Prepositions** are either **simple** or **complex.** Circle the instances of both sorts.

EXAMPLE   Marvin went (along with) us (to) the matinee.

9. They went into the haunted house with no fear.
10. Alongside the house was a garden whose barrenness was due to neglect; a weed patch would look good alongside of it.
11. As for the weather, we will have rain during the weekend.
12. In spite of the rain and despite any objections, we are going to the beach without any delay.
13. We left the fish on top of the refrigerator, but the cat jumped on the top of the counter and got it.
14. The guard in the lobby is of no use, with respect to crime prevention.

6.2   Prepositional Phrases and Other Structures   (Ref: CGCE 6.2)

DIRECTIONS   Rephrase the italicized *that*-clauses and infinitive clauses as prepositional phrases.

EXAMPLE   He was surprised *that she said that.*

He was surprised at her saying that.
_____

1. Applegate was conscious *that someone was there.*

_____

2. He is eager *to succeed.*

_____

3. They are ashamed *that they talked so loud.*

_____

4. She is careful *to watch for cars.*

_____

5. You are entitled *to receive a prize.*

_____

6. I am inclined *to prefer the red car.*

_____

7. The team was sorry *that it rained.*

_____

8. He strives *to make better grades.*

_____

9. We agreed *that we would follow a certain route.*

_____

10. She has heard *that there was a fire.*

_____

11. Someone told him *that there was to be a race.*

_____

12. The committee decided *to adjourn early.*

_____

6.3   Postposed Prepositions

(Ref: CGCE 6.3)

DIRECTIONS   Circle the **postposed prepositions.**

EXAMPLE   Which house did you leave it (at)?

1. What did he do that for?
2. Which shell did he put the pea under?
3. Laura is the friend whom he ran across in Paris.
4. It was a Norwegian ship that he sailed on.
5. The club he belongs to chartered a plane.
6. What I marvel at is the acrobat's skill.
7. What a deep hole she fell into!
8. The child was well cared for.
9. Mozart is pleasant to listen to.
10. I will go to sleep, whichever program you look at.
11. They have traveled the world over.
12. Who did they give the first prize to?

DIRECTIONS   Some of the sentences above have more formal variants with the preposition before its complement. Write those sentences with the preposition moved before its complement.

EXAMPLE   **At which house did you leave it?**

_____

_____

_____

_____

_____

_____

_____

6.4 Prepositions, Adverbs, and Modifiers   (Ref: CGCE 6.5, 46)

DIRECTIONS Some of the prepositions in the following sentences can be changed into **prepositional adverbs** by omitting their **complements.** Circle the prepositional complements that can be omitted. In some sentences there are none.

EXAMPLE A car drove past (the door).

1. A wild horse galloped by us.
2. The book was written by a ghost writer.
3. The doctor is in his office now.
4. He sat in the easy chair.
5. He had kippers for breakfast and has eaten nothing since then.
6. The boy joined his parents at the table and squeezed in between them.
7. If we can't get parsley, we'll have to do without it.
8. She's not doing anything in the garden, just walking about the place.
9. After briefly fainting, he came to consciousness again.
10. The main office is on the floor above this one.

DIRECTIONS Underline the words that modify prepositions or prepositional phrases.

EXAMPLE Now their footsteps could be heard <u>directly</u> over my head.

11. The mail arrived today shortly before noon.
12. He stopped just on the point of revealing his secret.
13. I left the newspaper right on the table.
14. He finished at two o'clock exactly.
15. She eats only with chopsticks.

6.5   Syntactic Functions of Prepositional Phrases   (Ref: CGCE 6.6)

DIRECTIONS   A prepositional phrase may function as an **adverbial** (A) adjunct, disjunct, or conjunct; **modifier of a noun phrase** (M); **complement of a verb** (CV); **complement of an adjective** (CA); or sometimes as a **nominal** (N) subject or complement of a preposition. Indicate the function of each italicized prepositional phrase by writing the appropriate abbreviation in the parentheses.

EXAMPLE   *To his surprise* (**A**), the people *on the bus* (**M**) depended *on him* (**CV**).

1. Paul is meditating *in the garden* (   ).

2. *Without doubt* (   ), the mayor will be reelected.

3. *In the first place* (   ), he's too young *for the roller coaster* (   ).

4. The ring *on her little finger* (   ) is an opal.

5. The neighbors *behind us* (   ) are looking *after the dog* (   ).

6. Felicia is afraid *of spiders* (   ).

7. *Across the street* (   ) is not too far.

8. *With a chuckle* (   ), the joker pulled the chair from *under him* (   ).

9. The boxer was eager *for a rematch* (   ).

10. Somebody *from the office* (   ) will check *on it* (   ).

11. She bought the picture *in the hall* (   ) *during her trip* (   ).

DIRECTIONS   Rewrite each sentence, adding to it prepositional phrases with the functions indicated in parentheses.

12. The policeman was suspicious. (modifier of noun; complement of adjective)

_____

13. The landlord disapproved. (adverbial; complement of verb)

_____

14. The trumpeter played. (adverbial; modifier of noun)

_____

6.6   Multiple Prepositional Phrases

(Ref: CGCE 6.6)

DIRECTIONS   Several prepositional phrases may occur together:

She lived *in the mountains during the summer with a friend.*
She sat *on the chair at the table in the back of the room.*

In the first sentence the three prepositional phrases are independent of one another. They are adverbials of place, time, and accompaniment, respectively, and can occur in any order: *She lived with a friend during the summer in the mountains,* for example. In the second sentence the four prepositional phrases are linked: *of the room* is a modifier of the noun phrase *the back; in the back of the room* similarly modifies *the table;* and *at the table in the back of the room* modifies *the chair.* The linked prepositional phrase *on the chair at the table in the back of the room* functions as an adverbial in the sentence. The prepositional phrases that are included in it cannot freely change their order; **She sat of the room in the back at the table on the chair* is nonsense. Some otherwise linked phrases can be made independent if they are separated from one another by commas in writing and by pauses in speech: *She sat on the chair, at the table, in the back of the room.* When they are so separated, the phrases can be reordered like any series of independent phrases: *She sat in the back of the room, at the table, on the chair.* Indicate whether the prepositional phrases in each sentence are independent of one another (I) or are linked modifiers (M), by writing the appropriate letter in the blanks.

1. Ask the man in the aisle seat of the third row of the balcony.   _____

2. Ask the man in the balcony, in the third row, in the aisle seat.   _____

3. He painted the house for his brother over a weekend.   _____

4. We're meeting at three o'clock in the afternoon.   _____

5. Chloris drove from Reno to Los Angeles in her convertible.   _____

6. Flora moved to Cairo in Illinois.   _____

7. Have you seen the picture in the centerfold of the magazine?   _____

8. The story of the man from La Mancha is widely known.   _____

9. The mirror in the bedroom, over the dresser, is cracked.   _____

10. The story in Sunday's paper about the riot was exaggerated.   _____

6.7   Prepositional Meanings   (Ref: CGCE 6.7–45)

DIRECTIONS   Supply an appropriate preposition for each blank. If no preposition is possible, put an X in the blank.

Place

1. He lives _____ Main Street _____ Terrytown and works _____ home.

2. He walked _____ the pool, climbed _____ the diving board, jumped _____ the water, and then went _____ home.

3. The squirrel leaped _____ the branch, _____ the tree, and ran _____ the forest.

4. Zeke left his hat _____ the table when he hid _____ the door.

5. Wilma strolled _____ the river, _____ the bridge, and _____ the meadow.

Cause, purpose, manner, source, means, agent, etc.

6. Milton bought a motorcycle _____ his wife _____ an ad he saw.

7. He gave a fly swatter _____ his mother _____ her vacation.

8. He got the idea _____ a novel to go canoeing _____ three friends.

9. We were surprised _____ his opposition _____ the plan.

10. The car was driven _____ a man _____ one eye.

11. _____ his mother's objection, he told her _____ the snake.

12. Everyone _____ Frieda makes a fire _____ matches.

13. _____ size, Watson is small _____ a wrestler.

14. It seems _____ me that, _____ Watson, we have no one to send.

Time

15. The visitors arrived _____ Friday _____ three o'clock _____ the afternoon.

16. They are going to stay _____ a week, _____ Friday _____ Thursday.

17. We have classes _____ noon; then, _____ lunch we study alone.

18. The mayor will be interviewed _____ next Tuesday _____ three and four o'clock.

19. Rip slept _____ all day, _____ supper time.

● 7.1   Simple and Complex Sentences   (Ref: CGCE 7.1)

DIRECTIONS   A **simple sentence** has only one **clause** (that is, one set of subject-verb elements). **Complex** and **compound sentences** have two or more clauses. Indicate which of the following sentences are simple (S) and which are complex or compound (C) by writing the appropriate symbol in the blank.

EXAMPLES	I quickly shut the door.	S
	I shut the door before the animal escaped.	C
	I shut the door, but the animal escaped.	C

1. Although James Bond is fictional, he is one of the world's most famous spies.   _____

2. He works for Her Majesty's Secret Service.   _____

3. Bond skis and skin-dives, and he plays baccarat.   _____

4. Among Bond's opponents were Dr. No and Goldfinger.   _____

5. He is noted for his relationships with beautiful women and arch-villains.   _____

6. While Bond was in Turkey, he made friends with a tribe of gypsies.   _____

7. The man who lay stretched out on his face beside the swimming pool might have been dead except for the slight movement of the grass below his open mouth.   _____

8. Bond did twenty slow pushups, prolonging each one so that his muscles had no rest.   _____

9. Breakfast was Bond's favorite meal of the day—two cups of strong black coffee without sugar, a single boiled egg in the dark blue egg cup with a gold ring around the top, two thick slices of whole-wheat toast, strawberry jam, marmalade, honey, and the *Times.*   _____

10. For ten minutes Bond gazed out across the minarets and mosques toward the dancing waves of the Bosphorus.   _____

11. He pressed the starter, and the Bentley roared into action.   _____

7.2   Clause Types

DIRECTIONS   There are seven basic clause types:

SVC	Mary is kind. Mary is a nurse.
SVA	Mary is in the house. The meeting was on Wednesday.
SV	The child was laughing.
SVO	Somebody caught the ball.
SVOC	We have proved him wrong. We have proved him a fool.
SVOA	I put the plate on the table. They scheduled the meeting on Monday.
SVOO	She gives me expensive presents.

Identify the clause type of each sentence by the appropriate abbreviation.

1. J. R. R. Tolkien wrote *The Lord of the Rings*.   _____

2. The story is about the Hobbits.   _____

3. All Hobbits are fat in the stomach.   _____

4. One of the Hobbits was Bilbo Baggins.   _____

5. Bilbo Baggins was at his door.   _____

6. I am the wizard Gandalf.   _____

7. Gandalf handed Bilbo a sealed note.   _____

8. Bilbo left his paraphernalia in the corner of the room.   _____

9. An odd-looking dwarf with a white beard blew smoke rings.   _____

10. Bilbo and the wizard wanted the magic ring.   _____

11. The creature Gollum followed them.   _____

12. Gollum's eyes flashed.   _____

13. People called the ancient dragon Smaug.   _____

14. Smaug kept his treasure safe.   _____

15. The dragon placed the ring among his treasures.   _____

16. Someone showed Bilbo the dragon's lair.   _____

17. The infuriated dragon roared.   _____

18. Gandalf appointed Bilbo keeper of the ring.   _____

19. The ring eventually proved a curse.   _____

20. The adventure of the ring was in an earlier age.   _____

7.3   Transformational Relations   (Ref: CGCE 7.5–6)

DIRECTIONS   Most *SVO* sentences have corresponding **passive** forms: *Many critics disliked the play* ~ *The play was disliked (by many critics)*. Write the passive equivalent of each sentence.

1. Captain James Kirk commands the U.S.S. *Enterprise.*

   _____

2. Lieutenant Uhura has contacted the Klingon ship.

   _____

3. Kirk considered Mr. Spock the most logical of the ship's company.

   _____

4. The science officer is asking the computer an unanswerable question.

   _____

5. Scotty may leave the tricorder in the engine room.

   _____

DIRECTIONS   An *SVOO* sentence can usually be related to an *SVOA* sentence in which a prepositional phrase corresponds to the indirect object: *She sent Jim a card* ~ *She sent a card to Jim*. Rephrase these sentences, replacing the indirect objects by prepositional phrases.

6. The Widow Wadman gave Uncle Toby a present.

   _____

7. Mr. Shandy did his wife a favor.

   _____

8. Mr. Yorick asked Susannah a simple question.

   _____

9. Tristram's name brought him a great deal of trouble.

   _____

10. Corporal Trim told Uncle Toby a story about the king of Bohemia.

   _____

7.4 Clause Elements   (Ref: CGCE 7.7–8)

DIRECTIONS Pick out each **subject** (S), **verb** (V), **direct object** (Od), **indirect object** (Oi), **subject complement** (Cs), **object complement** (Co), and **adverbial** (A), by writing the appropriate abbreviation in parentheses. Be prepared to explain what syntactic signals identify each element.

1. Mame Dennis (   ) lives (   ) at No. 3 Beekman Place (   ). 2. Mame (   ) became (   ) the guardian of her orphaned nephew, Patrick (   ). 3. Eventually (   ), she and Beauregard Jackson Picket Burnside (   ) were married (   ) at his plantation (   ). 4. First (   ) she (   ) proved (   ) herself (   ) a skilled horsewoman (   ). 5. Mame and Vera Charles (   ) are taking (   ) poor Agnes Gooch (   ) under their wing (   ). 6. They (   ) gave (   ) Agnes (   ) advice about life (   ). 7. Agnes's adventure (   ) was (   ) exciting (   ) for six months (   ). 8. Patrick (   ) was finding (   ) life with Mame (   ) too hectic (   ). 9. During his brief engagement to a WASP from Mountebank (   ), Mame (   ) introduced (   ) the young man (   ) to Pegeen Ryan (   ). 10. The irrepressible Mame (   ) has promised (   ) her great-nephew (   ) a trip to India (   ).

DIRECTIONS These sentences are ambiguous. For each, identify two clause types (*SVOC, SVOO,* etc.) that the sentence might be. Be prepared to paraphrase each sentence in two ways to show the different meanings.

11. The Romans built this way.   _____ _____
12. She made him a mess.   _____ _____
13. The butcher weighed 98 pounds.   _____ _____
14. The buzzer sounded loud and clear.   _____ _____
15. This man can save you the best.   _____ _____
16. Alice found him a puzzle.   _____ _____
17. My doctor gives the poorest free treatment.   _____ _____
18. Call me fast.   _____ _____
19. Her hobby is destroying all her friends.   _____ _____
20. The mayor appointed an assistant chief of police.   _____ _____

7.5 Semantic Roles   (Ref: CGCE 7.9)

DIRECTIONS   Four typical **semantic roles** of clause elements are **agentive** (one who causes the event), **affected** (person or thing directly involved in the event other than as causer), **recipient** (one who is passively related to the event), and **attribute** (which describes or identifies some participant in the event). Identify the role of each italicized element by writing the appropriate term in the parentheses after it.

1. *Beowulf* (   ) killed *the monster Grendel* (   ) in hand-to-hand combat.
2. *King Hygelac* (   ) offered *Beowulf* (   ) *a reward of gold rings* (   ).
3. Later Beowulf became *the king of the Geats* (   ).
4. *The brave king* (   ) made *his people* (   ) *famous* (   ) throughout Scandinavia.
5. Of all men, he was *the gentlest and most eager for praise* (   ).

DIRECTIONS   A **current attribute** denotes an already existing characteristic; a **resulting attribute** denotes a characteristic that comes about because of the event reported in the sentence. Put parentheses around the complements and indicate whether each is current or resulting.

6. He is a champion wrestler. _____
7. The most skillful wrestler will become champion. _____
8. Grendel pulled free. _____
9. But he found Beowulf very strong. _____
10. Beowulf made the kingdom safe. _____
11. The Danes drank their mead warm. _____
12. They brewed their mead strong. _____
13. Grendel's Dam got angry. _____
14. She looked demonic. _____
15. Beowulf likes his sword sharp. _____

7.6   Subject Roles

(Ref: CGCE 7.9–13)

DIRECTIONS   The subject of a clause may have various roles:

agentive:	*John* opened the door with the key. *My dog* was walking.
instrumental:	*The key* opened the door. *An avalanche* destroyed the house.
affected:	*The door* opened. *The flowers* died. *I* got angry.
recipient:	*His son* has a radio. *He* saw the accident. *I* liked the play.
locative:	*The path* is swarming with ants. *The bus* holds forty people.
temporal:	*Tomorrow* is my birthday. *Last winter* was mild.
eventive:	*The concert* is on Thursday.
empty:	*It* is raining.

Put parentheses around the subject of each sentence and identify its role.

1. The astronaut flew his ship to the moon by rocket power. _____

2. Rocket power flew the ship to the moon. _____

3. The ship flew to the moon. _____

4. NASA gave that university some moon rocks. _____

5. That university owns some moon rocks. _____

6. It is lonely in space. _____

7. Space is lonely. _____

8. Tomorrow is the launch. _____

9. The launch is tomorrow. _____

10. Apollo 17 was the last spaceship of its series. _____

11. Neil Armstrong stepped onto the moon's surface. _____

12. The Apollo 17's module landed on a lunar plain. _____

13. It is desolate of all life on the moon. _____

14. Each of the Apollo vehicles has held three astronauts. _____

15. One astronaut saw some orange-colored soil. _____

16. Lunar vehicles have explored the surface of the moon. _____

17. Scientists have over six hundred pounds of lunar rock. _____

18. Geologists are studying the moon rocks. _____

19. The return of Apollo 17 marked the end of the program. _____

20. 1980 may be the year of the first manned flight to Mars. _____

7.7 Object Roles and Subject Priorities   (Ref: CGCE 7.9, 14–17)

DIRECTIONS   The direct and indirect objects of a clause may have various roles:

affected Od: John opened *the door*. I was walking *my dog*.
effected Od: Baird invented *television*. She sang *a song*. He took *a nap*.
locative Od: The horse jumped *the fence*.
recipient Oi (affected Od):   He gave *his wife* a bracelet.
affected Oi (effected Od):   He gave *the door* a kick.

Put parentheses around the indirect object and around the direct object and identify their roles.

1. Felix Wankel designed the first rotary power system.   _____

2. A Japanese firm first commercially produced the product.   _____

3. The alumni gave the quarterback a rotary-engine sports car. _____

   _____

4. They sat him in the driver's seat.   _____

5. The car can comfortably drive the roughest roads.   _____

6. The car hit a ditch.   _____

7. A dealer can service the new engine.   _____

8. A skilled mechanic can give the new engine good service.   _____

   _____

DIRECTIONS   Rewrite the sentences, making the changes called for in parentheses and any other necessary ones. Note any change in the subject role.

9. Druella is growing nightshade in the garden. (omit the agentive)

_____

10. The full moon changes her husband into a werewolf. (omit the instrument)

_____

11. She stains her lips dark purple with belladonna. (omit the agentive)

_____

12. Henbane is growing over the path. (use the locative as subject)

_____

13. Midnight is the gathering of the coven. (use the eventive as subject)

_____

7.8　Summary of Roles (1)　　　　　　　(Ref: CGCE 7.9–17)

tions are used: affected, agentive, current attribute, effected, empty subject, instru-
by writing the appropriate letter in front of the example. (The following abbreviations are used: affected, agentive, current attribute, effected, empty subject, instrumental, intensive verb, intransitive verb, locative, monotransitive verb, recipient,
resulting attribute, temporal.)

		S	V	C
1. _____	He became an old man.	a. aff	inten	cur
2. _____	He stood still.	b. aff	inten	res
3. _____	He turned traitor.	c. agen	inten	cur
4. _____	It's rainy.	d. agen	inten	res
5. _____	New York gets crowded.	e. loc	inten	res
6. _____	She's lovely.	f. temp	inten	cur
7. _____	Yesterday was cooler.	g. emp	inten	cur

		S	V
8. _____	It snowed.	a. aff	intr
9. _____	She knits.	b. agen	intr
10. _____	The bubble burst.	c. inst	intr
11. _____	The pencil-sharpener works.	d. emp	intr

		S	V	O
12. _____	He's got a caftan.	a. agen	mono	aff
13. _____	He swam the channel.	b. inst	mono	aff
14. _____	He played the piano.	c. reci	mono	aff
15. _____	He took a walk.	d. agen	mono	reci
16. _____	He gave a hiccup.	e. inst	mono	reci
17. _____	A saw will cut the board.	f. agen	mono	loc
18. _____	The room accommodates thirty.	g. loc	mono	aff
19. _____	Seat belts benefit everybody.	h. agen	mono	eff
20. _____	He endowed the college.	i. aff	mono	eff

7.9 Summary of Roles (2) (Ref: CGCE 7.9–17)

DIRECTIONS Within each clause type, match the examples with the semantic roles by writing the appropriate letter in front of the example. (The following abbreviations are used: affected, agentive, complex transitive verb, current attribute, ditransitive verb, effected, eventive, instrumental, intensive verb, locative, recipient, resulting attribute.)

	S	V	A
1. ___ He is under the house.	a. aff	inten	loc
2. ___ Supper will be outdoors.	b. agen	inten	loc
3. ___ They stayed inside.	c. ev	inten	loc

	S	V	O	C
4. ___ They elected him president.	a. agen	comp	aff	cur
5. ___ The food made him sleepy.	b. agen	comp	aff	res
6. ___ She finds him amusing.	c. inst	comp	aff	res
7. ___ She brewed the coffee too strong.	d. reci	comp	aff	cur
8. ___ He drinks his coffee hot.	e. agen	comp	eff	res

	S	V	O	A
9. ___ She put the book away.	a. agen	comp	aff	loc
10. ___ She wants it on the table.	b. inst	comp	aff	loc
11. ___ An umbrella knocked his hat off.	c. reci	comp	aff	loc

	S	V	Oi	Od
12. ___ I sent her a card.	a. agen	ditr	reci	aff
13. ___ The thunder gave me a start.	b. agen	ditr	aff	aff
14. ___ I asked her a question.	c. inst	ditr	reci	eff

	S	V	Oi	Od	C
15. ___ He bought me a car secondhand.	a. agen	ditr	reci	aff	cur
16. ___ We made us some coffee fresh.	b. agen	ditr	reci	eff	res
17. ___ We elected us Bob president.	c. agen	ditr	reci	eff	res

7.10 Subject-Verb Concord (1) (Ref: CGCE 7.18–26)

DIRECTIONS If a verb has variable forms (such as *sing/sings* or *am/are*), the form **agrees** with its subject in number and person, although the agreement is sometimes with the form of the subject (**grammatical concord**) and sometimes with the meaning of the subject (**notional concord**). Circle the form of the verb that is most appropriate. In some sentences, more than one form is possible; choose the one that seems best.

1. This broadcast of the Olympic games *is / are* being transmitted by satellite.
2. The 1972 Olympics *was / were* held in Munich.
3. Sports *occupies / occupy* the full time of many of the "amateurs."
4. Whether this year's games *was / were* going to be held *was / were* doubtful.
5. To participate in friendly rivalries *is / are* what athletes come for.
6. What the participants *wants / want* *is / are* to win.
7. What *was / were* the most exciting sports last Olympics *is / are* not so this year.
8. The American swimming team *is / are* not the same this year.
9. The team *has / have* taken their places on the starting blocks.
10. Gymnastics *is / are* among the most graceful of the sports.
11. The government *has / have* arranged visas for all the visiting teams.
12. The board of governors *has / have* been unable to agree.
13. "The Stars and Stripes Forever" *is / are* being played now.
14. A fanfare of trumpets and a parade *opens / open* the events.
15. The police *is / are* guarding the arena.
16. Track and field *is / are* the favorite event of many.
17. Both professional and amateur behavior *is / are* exhibited.
18. Either a Russian or one of the Japanese *is / are* likely to win.
19. Neither of the boxers *looks / look* tired.
20. Either of them *has / have* a chance of winning.
21. The noise and excitement *is / are* what *keeps / keep* our attention.
22. The biggest medal-winner and the greatest swimmer *was / were* Spitz.

7.11   Subject-Verb Concord (2)   (Ref: CGCE 7.18—26)

DIRECTIONS   As in the preceding exercise, circle the form of the verb that seems most appropriate.

1. None of the excitement *has / have* gone out of the games.
2. None of the participants *has / have* been bored.
3. Everyone among the athletes *wants / want* to perform perfectly.
4. All *is / are* the best and most highly trained.
5. All *is / are* nervous expectation in the athletes' quarters.
6. A number of shot-putters *is / are* practicing on the field.
7. The number of wrestlers *is / are* too great for the time scheduled.
8. More than one golden lad *has / have* tasted the dust of defeat.
9. More than one *has / have* scored surprise upsets.
10. One out of four contestants *was / were* in the last Olympics too.
11. Each of the games *has / have* importance for the whole contest.
12. No one other than the Russians *wins / win* many women's events.
13. There *is / are* an Australian and a Pole in the ring now.
14. There's / There're going to be a Swede and a Czech boxing next.
15. Either the referee or I *is / am / are* going to have to get new glasses.
16. The losing wrestler and I *is / am / are* agreed about the referee.
17. It is I who *is / am* best able to judge.
18. It's me who *is / am* best able to judge.
19. *The Canterbury Tales is / are* Chaucer's most famous work.
20. *The Canterbury Tales includes / include* many stories in verse.
21. Here *is / are* your hat and coat.
22. Every man and every woman *has / have* an equal vote.
23. The inside of the boxes *was / were* covered with wallpaper.
24. Each of us *has / have* the same chance in the contest.
25. There *is / are* some problems ahead of us.
26. There *is / are* a crowd of people outside trying to get in.

7.12   Subject-Complement and Pronoun Concord   (Ref: CGCE 7.27–30)

DIRECTIONS   A noun subject complement usually agrees in number with the subject, and an object complement with the object. There are, however, some exceptions. Fill the blank with an appropriate form, singular or plural, of the noun phrase in parentheses.

1. Fischer defeated Spassky to become _____. (world champion)
2. Fischer and Spassky are both _____. (grandmaster)
3. Fischer and Spassky were each _____ in their respective countries. (the best player)
4. Chess-players are _____. (an odd sort)
5. After the match, Fischer was _____ with Spassky. (a friend)
6. What Spassky needed was _____. (four more points)
7. Those "ivory" chess pieces are _____. (a fake)
8. Fischer and Spassky were _____. (a good match)
9. The last seven games were _____ to watch. (a pleasure)
10. The referee declared Fischer _____ of the match. (the winner)

DIRECTIONS   Fill the blank with a pronoun referring to the italicized noun phrase.

11. Aaron Burr disliked *Mr. Hamilton* and therefore shot _____.
12. *Paolo and Francesca* killed _____ for love.
13. *None of the skiers* had _____ skis on.
14. *None of the news* had _____ usual effect.
15. *Everybody* believes _____ ought to be able to arrange things to suit _____.
16. —There was *someone* on the phone for you. —What did _____ want?
17. If *anybody* has trouble filling out _____ income-tax forms, _____ can come to the Tax Office, where a clerk will help _____.
18. *No one* is allowed to be by _____ in that commune.
19. *Either Jack or Jill* will have to watch _____ step.

7.13 Vocatives

(Ref: CGCE 7.31–32)

DIRECTIONS A **vocative** indicates the person or persons to whom a sentence is addressed. It is usually set off from the remainder of the sentence with commas. Add commas to the sentences where they are called for to set off the vocatives. Be prepared to discuss what attitude each vocative implies the speaker has toward the addressee.

EXAMPLE   John, I want you.

1. Felix Randal what have you been doing?
2. You said a mouthful Queen.
3. I hear Mr. Borden that your daughter wants to join Woodsmen of the World.
4. Mary this is John.
5. We are gathered dearly beloved to join this man and this woman in holy wedlock.
6. Get out of my chair meathead.
7. You in the back row break it up.
8. Close the window young man will you?
9. Close the window you.
10. Anyone who finds the note in this bottle notify the Coast Guard at once.
11. Brother of mine where are you going?
12. Stop teasing that monkey the two of you.
13. O wind if Winter comes, can Spring be far behind?
14. Cars you better not get in that truck's way.

DIRECTIONS In what ways do vocatives differ from the noun phrases that can serve as subjects?

15. _____

_____

_____

7.14 Negation (1)

(Ref: CGCE 7.33–34)

DIRECTIONS The **negative** form of a sentence is usually made by putting *not* between the operator and the predication. Write the negative of each sentence; in some an operator must be added.

1. Navajo blankets have been popular among tourists.

   _____

2. Nineteenth-century blankets are in especially great demand.

   _____

3. Artists like Georgia O'Keefe collect such woven goods.

   _____

4. Navajo women learned weaving from their Pueblo neighbors.

   _____

5. The blankets have many practical uses.

   _____

DIRECTIONS Some operators can contract with the subject (*he's*), and *not* can contract with most operators (*isn't*). Thus, two forms of negation are possible for many sentences, with different **contractions.** Write the possible contracted forms of each of the sentences.

6. They are dribbling. _____

7. She had schussed the slope. _____

8. He will sclaff again. _____

9. He would birdie it. _____

10. She has snookered him. _____

11. I have been sculling. _____

12. I am getting clipped. _____

7.15   Nonassertive Forms
and Negative Intensification

(Ref: CGCE 7.35–36)

DIRECTIONS   **Assertive** forms like *some, somehow, sometimes, somewhat, already, too,* and *still* are usually replaced in negative clauses by **nonassertive** forms like *any, in any way, ever, at all, yet, either,* and *any more.* Write the negative forms of the sentences, using nonassertive forms wherever appropriate.

1. He wants some soy sauce.   _____

2. We can get tempura somewhere.   _____

3. She still likes sukiyaki.   _____

4. They have teriyaki too.   _____

5. The rice is seasoned somewhat.   _____

DIRECTIONS   Write the **positive** form of the sentences, using assertive forms wherever appropriate.

6. I don't much like jellyfish.   _____

7. We don't ever eat raw fish.   _____

8. It doesn't taste good at all.   _____

9. They haven't had tea yet.   _____

10. Supper isn't lasting long.   _____

DIRECTIONS   Negatives can be **intensified** in various ways, for example by adding expressions like *at all* or *whatever.* Rephrase each of these sentences to intensify the negative. Do each sentence in a different way.

11. They have nowhere to go now.   _____

12. We haven't seen anyone yet.   _____

13. I had never thought of it before. _____

14. There is no ticket available.   _____

15. He won't eat.   _____

7.16   Negation (2)   ˙(Ref: CGCE 7.37–39)

DIRECTIONS   Rewrite each sentence, following the directions in parentheses and making any other needed changes.

1. Don't ask me any questions. (Negate the direct object instead of the predication.) _____

2. A map won't show that town. (Negate the subject instead of the predication.) _____

3. You can't find a friendlier goldfish anywhere. (Negate the adverbial of place instead of the predication, and move it to initial position.) _____
   _____

4. Nobody ever promised either one of them any help. (Make the sentence affirmative by changing *nobody* to *somebody*.)
   _____

5. He said that something concerning some of us was already happening. (Make the predication negative by adding *not* before *said*.)
   _____
   _____

6. Few students will be affected much by the new blue laws. (Change *few* to *many*.) _____
   _____

7. Something has surprised me quite a bit. (Add *seldom* at the beginning of the sentence.) _____

8. I forgot to put any salt on it at all. (Change *forgot* to *remembered*.)
   _____

9. The woman lying on the piano hasn't ever joined in the singing. (Negate the adverbial of time instead of the predication and move it into initial position.) _____
   _____

10. She was unaware of anyone waiting. (Change *unaware* to *aware*.)
   _____

11. We have still told no one the secret. (Negate the predication instead of the indirect object.) _____

7.17 Scope of Negation

(Ref: CGCE 7.40–42)

DIRECTIONS Show the **scope** of the negation in these sentences by putting parentheses around the part of the sentence that is negated. Some sentences have two negatives; indicate the scope of each. Words printed in SMALL CAPITALS have nuclear (that is, especially prominent) stress on them.

1. It obviously isn't too late to go.
2. It isn't obviously too late to go.
3. I almost didn't finish reading the book.
4. I didn't almost finish reading the book.
5. He hasn't made a decision without DOUBT.
6. He hasn't made a DECISION, without DOUBT.
7. She isn't ANSWERING the questions, CERTAINLY.
8. She isn't answering the questions CERTAINLY.
9. We didn't ask any of the questions she expected.
10. We didn't ask some of the questions she expected.
11. Not a student finished on time.
12. A student didn't finish on time.
13. They have not seen him studying.
14. They have seen him not studying.
15. They didn't get married because they just LIKE each other.
16. They didn't get MARRIED, because they just LIKE each other.
17. All the movies at that theater aren't fit for CHILDREN to see.
18. ALL the movies at that theater aren't fit for CHILDREN to see.
19. The Dean said we may not build a bonfire, because it may not be safe.
20. It must not be cold, because the cat won't stay indoors.
21. You shouldn't go on working so hard, because you can't finish anyway.
22. You needn't look so worried just because you oughtn't to have kept us waiting.
23. I'll bet you can't stand in the corner and not think about a white bear.
24. You mayn't not eat. (i.e., 'You must eat.')

7.18   Focus of Negation   (Ref: CGCE 7.41)

DIRECTIONS   Show the **focus** of the negation in these sentences by underlining the words that would have a special nuclear stress in order to imply the information in parentheses.

1. Guy Fawkes didn't intend to blow up Westminster. (He did it accidentally.)
2. Guy Fawkes didn't intend to blow up Westminster. (Somebody else did.)
3. Guy Fawkes didn't intend to blow up Westminster. (He was aiming at St. Paul's.)
4. Guy Fawkes didn't intend to blow up Westminster. (He wanted to burn it down.)
5. Guy Fawkes didn't intend to blow up Westminster. (No matter who says he did.)
6. Adolphe Sax wasn't the inventor of the sousaphone. (Sax invented the saxophone, and John Philip Sousa the sousaphone.)
7. All the cameras aren't working. (None of them are.)
8. All the cameras aren't working. (Some of them are.)

DIRECTIONS   What is the implication of the negation focus, as shown by the location of a special nuclear stress (small capitals)?

9. He isn't going to the movie because it is X-RATED.

_____

10. He isn't going to the MOVIE because it is X-RATED.

_____

11. Dale hit Leslie, but she didn't KICK him.

_____

12. Dale hit Leslie, but SHE didn't kick HIM.

_____

7.19 Statements, Questions, Commands, Exclamations

(Ref: CGCE 7.43–44)

DIRECTIONS Indicate whether each sentence is **declarative** (D), **interrogative** (Q), **imperative** (I), or **exclamatory** (E) in form by writing the appropriate letter in the blank. The form of a sentence may differ from the intent of its speaker. For instance, *I wonder who she is* is a statement in form, but a question in meaning. Be prepared to discuss which of these sentences have implied meanings that differ from their form.

1. Why are you so edgy tonight, Mother? _____
2. Don't bother your mother, Carol. _____
3. She got arrested at the police-brutality protest because she brutalized an officer. _____
4. The cops'll get you for that, Walter. _____
5. Florida, we'll have dinner now. _____
6. Will you serve it in here, please? _____
7. Who knows when our crusade will succeed? _____
8. How sweet it will be. _____
9. How sweet will it be? _____
10. Just double my pay, and watch the justice flow. _____
11. Florida, don't be crass. _____
12. What materialistic notions you have. _____

DIRECTIONS Identify each question as a *yes-no* **question** (YN), a *wh-* **question** (WH), or an **alternative question** (A), depending on whether the expected answer is *yes* or *no,* an item of information not presented by the questioner, or a choice among options presented by the questioner. An acute accent (´) signals a rising tone of voice, a grave accent (`) a falling tone.

13. Did the Wife of Bath have fóur husbands or five? _____
14. Was her name Álison? _____
15. Why was the Wife of Bath going on pìlgrimage? _____
16. What kind of hùsband did Alison want? _____
17. Would you say she was a women's líbber? _____
18. Do you suppose Alison would rather be dominated by a húsband or be independently sìngle? _____

7.20 Yes-No Questions   (Ref: CGCE 7.45–47, 51)

DIRECTIONS   Write the *yes-no* **question** that corresponds to each of the following statements and is least biased with respect to an answer.

1. Charlie Brown is going to be manager of the team again this year.

   _____

2. Charlie's team hasn't ever won a game.

   _____

3. Charlie always has hope for the new season.

   _____

4. Snoopy has already decided to play shortstop.

   _____

5. Someone can get Peppermint Patty to coach the team.

   _____

6. Lucy likes to play in the outfield.

   _____

7. They may have learned something from last season.

   _____

DIRECTIONS   How do the following questions differ from one another in the assumptions that underlie them?

8. Has Charlie Brown ever succeeded at anything?
9. Has Charlie Brown sometimes succeeded at something?
10. Hasn't Charlie Brown ever succeeded at anything?
11. Hasn't Charlie Brown sometimes succeeded at something?

_____

_____

_____

7.21   Tag Questions and Declarative Questions   (Ref: CGCE 7.48–50)

DIRECTIONS   **Tag questions** like *do they?* and *isn't it?* echo the subject and operator of the main clause, but usually reverse the negative polarity. Add a tag question to each sentence.

1. Hamlet was indecisive, _____

2. Uncle Claudius had murdered Hamlet's father, _____

3. Queen Gertrude shouldn't have married her husband's brother, _____

4. Polonius knew a lot of aphorisms, _____

5. Elsinore couldn't have been a very quiet place, _____

DIRECTIONS   Describe the difference in meaning between the sentences of each pair. An acute accent (′) and a question mark signal a rising tone of voice; a grave accent (‵) and a period signal a falling tone.

6. a. Zenith is one of the great cities of the Midwèst, ísn't it?

   b. Zenith isn't one of the great cities of the Midwèst, ís it?

   _____

   _____

7. a. George Babbitt is a typical American bùsinessman, ísn't he?

   b. George Babbitt is a typical American bùsinessman, ìsn't he.

   _____

   _____

8. a. You think you're better than George Bàbbitt, dón't you?

   b. You think you're better than George Bàbbitt, dó you?

   _____

   _____

9. a. Have you been to the Bóosters' Club yet?

   b. You have been to the Bóosters' Club already?

   _____

   _____

7.22   *Wh-* Questions   (Ref: CGCE 7.52–53)

DIRECTIONS   For each statement, write a corresponding *wh-* question in which an **interrogative word** replaces the italicized expression.

1. The Bunkers live *in New York City.*

   _____

2. The Bunkers live in *the* city *of New York.*

   _____

3. Archie is *Edith's husband.*

   _____

4. *After their marriage,* Mike and Gloria moved in with Archie.

   _____

5. Mike sometimes sits in *Archie's* chair.

   _____

6. Mike and Archie quarrel *because they have different political views.*

   _____

7. Archie *never* admits he is wrong.

   _____

8. Archie brought home *a burglar alarm.*

   _____

9. The alarm did *not* work *very well.*

   _____

10. The alarm did *not* work *very* well.

    _____

11. Mike has· been at the university *for some years.*

    _____

12. Archie likes to *watch television* in the evenings.

    _____

13. Mike eats *a great deal.*

    _____

7.23 Alternative Questions (Ref: CGCE 7.54–55)

DIRECTIONS Combine each set of questions into a single **alternative question.**

EXAMPLE Would you like chocolate? Would you like vanilla?

Would you like chocolate or vanilla?

or **Which would you like—chocolate or vanilla?**

1. Do you read palms? Do you read head bumps?

2. Is the life line longer? Is the heart line longer?

3. Does this bump show intelligence? Does this bump not show intelligence?

4. Is a phrenologist the same as a palmist? Isn't he the same as a palmist?

5. Does the right hand show the future? Does the left hand show the future?

6. Can phrenology be a science? Is it a superstition?

DIRECTIONS Explain how the questions in each pair differ in implication.

7. a. Shall we serve coffee or TÉA? b. Shall we serve CÓFFEE or TÈA?

8. a. Was JÍM working or JÒHN? b. Was JÍM working, or JÓHN?

9. a. Are you going to HÉLP? b. Are you going to HÉLP or ÀREN'T you?

7.24 Exclamatory and Rhetorical Questions (Ref: CGCE 7.56–57)

DIRECTIONS For each statement write two corresponding **exclamatory questions**—one negative and one positive.

EXAMPLE It is getting dark.
Isn't it getting dark! 'Is 'it getting dark!

1. It is sweet.

2. He will try.

3. We have been clever.

4. She sings.

5. I am lucky.

DIRECTIONS What statement is implied by each **rhetorical question?**

EXAMPLE When will the rain stop?
I hope the rain will stop soon.

6. If winter comes, can spring be far behind?

7. What is worse than a thankless child?

8. Where can we find an honest man?

9. Isn't anyone going to volunteer?

10. How can you not agree with us?

7.25　Commands

(Ref: CGCE 7.58–62)

DIRECTIONS　For each statement, write a corresponding **imperative sentence.** Words in small capitals are stressed and should be retained in the command.

EXAMPLE　You will jump now.　　**Jump now.** _____

1. You will make me a pastrami sandwich.

   _____

2. You should not be looking out the window while you slice the meat.

   _____

3. You will add some horseradish, please.

   _____

4. YOU will take your hand out of the pickle jar.

   _____

5. Everyone will have something to eat.

   _____

6. Moe will take the orders and Bridget will serve.

   _____

7. Bernie, YOU will stay out of the way.

   _____

8. We will all do our best.

   _____

9. The music will begin.

   _____

10. The customers must not leave.

    _____

11. We will not be late.

    _____

12. You will sing for us. (persuasive or insistent)

    _____

7.26   Exclamations

(Ref: CGCE 7.63)

DIRECTIONS   For each statement, write a corresponding **exclamatory sentence** in which the italicized expression becomes the exclamatory *wh-* element.

EXAMPLE   There was *a crowd* at the game.

What a crowd there was at the game!

1. That was *a lucky interception*.

_____

2. That interception was *lucky*.

_____

3. They've called time out *often*.

_____

4. They are in *a mess*.

_____

5. He *can run*.

_____

DIRECTIONS   There are several ways of showing an emotional reaction other than the exclamatory sentence patterns beginning with *what* and *how*, as in *What a long time it lasted! How long a time it lasted!* What means are used in the following sentences to show exclamation or emphasis?

6. It lasted a long time!

_____

7. It lasted a l-o-o-o-n-g time.

_____

8. It lasted a long, long, long time.

_____

9. It lasted such an incredibly long time.

_____

118

7.27 Formulas and Aphoristic Sentences (Ref: CGCE 7.64–65)

DIRECTIONS Some minor types of sentences are very productive, so that it is easy to make up new sentences with the same pattern. Others are so limited that it may be difficult to think of another sentence of the same type. For as many of the following as you can, make up a similar sentence.

1. Off with her head. _____

2. So far, so good. _____

3. The more, the merrier. _____

4. Least said, soonest mended. _____

5. Easy come, easy go. _____

6. Like father, like son. _____

7. Another day, another dollar. _____

8. Better you than me. _____

9. How come you're so sure? _____

10. No fair doing that. _____

11. No coward, he. _____

12. What, me worry? _____

13. What's to get excited about? _____

14. Why not relax? _____

15. How about a movie? _____

16. If only we'd waited! _____

17. To think you might have been a podiatrist! _____
_____

18. Oh for some company! _____

19. Him and his books! _____

20. Now for a drink! _____

21. Far be it from me to criticize. _____

22. Suffice it to say she left. _____

23. May all your days be happy. _____

24. Long live the Queen. _____

25. The Lord help you. _____

7.28 Block Language (Ref: CGCE 7.66)

DIRECTIONS Expand each example of **block language** into a complete sentence by adding any missing clause elements and closed-system words.

1. FACULTY AND GRADUATE STUDENT LOUNGE

_____

2. SLOW—CHILDREN CROSSING

_____

3. IN CASE OF FIRE ONLY

_____

4. ALL THE NEWS THAT'S FIT TO PRINT

_____

5. POISON

_____

6. !! SALE OF THE CENTURY !!

_____

7. EVERYTHING YOU ALWAYS WANTED TO KNOW ABOUT SEX —BUT WERE AFRAID TO ASK

_____

DIRECTIONS Very informal conversation may have some of the characteristics of block language. Expand the following into full sentences.

8. —Finished? —Almost. —How much longer? —Ten minutes.

_____

_____

9. —Lunch? —Sure, what? —Tuna. —Ugh. —OK, eggs.

_____

_____

10. [phone rings] —Yes? —Mr. Johnson? —No. —Sorry, wrong number.

_____

_____

7.29   Headline English   (Ref: CGCE 7.66)

DIRECTIONS   **Headline English** is a special style of block language that not only omits major clause elements and close-system words, but also condenses grammatical structure by using phrases where clauses would be more explicit. The result is sometimes potentially ambiguous. Expand each of these ambiguous headlines into two sentences of different meanings.

1. RED DEFECTOR BELIEVED IN U.S.

   _____

   _____

2. MYTHS OF AGING HUMOROUSLY SHOWN

   _____

   _____

3. THIRD BIRTHDAY PARTY TODAY

   _____

   _____

4. SHE'S UPSET WINNER (under a photograph)

   _____

   _____

5. OFFENSIVE LINEMAN (under a photograph)

   _____

   _____

6. RESIGNED DEAN OF HUMANITIES GOES TO PARSONS COLLEGE

   _____

   _____

7. REDS FAVOR CONTROL OF SPACE TALKS

   _____

   _____

8. ANTIQUE STRIPPER TO DEMONSTRATE WARES

   _____

   _____

● 8.1   Adverbial Structures and Positions   (Ref: CGCE 8.1, 3)

DIRECTIONS   Underline the **adverbials,** and identify each as a noun phrase (NP), a prepositional phrase (PP), a finite verb clause (FC), a nonfinite verb clause (NC), a verbless clause (VC), or an adverb phrase (AP)—an adverb alone (*soon*) or a group of words with an adverb as head (*very soon*)—by writing the appropriate abbreviation in the blank.

1. Albert plays the timpani with the Tucson Symphony Orchestra.   _____

2. However, the bongo drums are his real love.   _____

3. They have no bongo player because few symphonies use bongos.   _____

4. Albert has been studying the cello recently.   _____

5. To play the cello, you have to take lessons.   _____

6. He plays the bongo drums more often than the cello.   _____

7. The bongos have great potential when played by an expert.   _____

8. You have to hold the bongos this way.   _____

9. The conductor, ever open to new ideas, added bongos.   _____

10. Growing impatient, the audience began to fidget.   _____

DIRECTIONS   Underline the adverbials and identify the position of each as **initial** (I = before the subject), **medial** (M = between subject and verb; or, if there are auxiliaries, M1 = before an auxiliary, or M2 = after all auxiliaries), or **final** (F = after the verb, object, or complement).

12. The home team probably won.   _____

11. Probably the home team will win.   _____

13. The home team probably will win.   _____

14. The home team will probably win.   _____

15. The home team will win probably.   _____

16. Suddenly, the pitcher threw the ball to the shortstop.   _____ _____

17. Apparently he once pitched a perfect game.   _____ _____

18. Nora has never hiked in the Rockies.   _____ _____

19. She really is paddling the canoe this time.   _____ _____

20. Before they finish, they will certainly have tried.   _____ _____

8.2   Viewpoint Adjuncts and Intensifiers   (Ref: CGCE 8.7, 12–18)

DIRECTIONS   Underline each **viewpoint adjunct.**

EXAMPLE   To tap a telephone is not <u>technically</u> a difficult operation.

1. The new plan was not practical economically.
2. Men can theoretically travel to the stars.
3. Scientifically, myths are poor explanations of nature.
4. Taxwise, the government depends on middle-income citizens.
5. Linguistically speaking, Englishmen and Americans are growing closer together.
6. Gymnastics is a great sport, from the observer's standpoint.

DIRECTIONS   Underline each **intensifier,** and indicate whether it is an **emphasizer** (E), an **amplifier** (A), or a **downtoner** (D) by writing the appropriate letter in the blank.

EXAMPLE   I <u>honestly</u> don't know what he wants.   **E**

7. We deeply appreciate your help.   _____
8. The team is simply losing every game it plays.   _____
9. The Smiths have traveled a little.   _____
10. He believed the story completely.   _____
11. Jason all but left Medea at the temple door.   _____
12. We definitely need a larger room.   _____
13. The doctor more or less said Throckmorton was well.   _____
14. I'll write that paper tomorrow for sure.   _____
15. She fully intends to finish on time.   _____
16. Albert doesn't object to shrimp in the slightest.   _____

8.3   Focusing Adjuncts   (Ref: CGCE 8.8–11)

DIRECTIONS   Circle each **focusing adjunct**, and underline the part of the sentence that is focused.

EXAMPLES   We bought some beer (as well). (as well as soft drinks)

We bought some beer (as well). (as well as brought some along)

1. Only a jet can travel that fast.
2. The foreman in particular was eager to finish.
3. Even Roger is writing his senator.
4. Roger is writing his congressman as well. (as well as his senator)
5. We are staying mainly in Scandinavia.
6. They wrote us just a short note.
7. Only the boys were catching frogs.
8. The boys were only catching frogs. (not fish)
9. The boys were only catching frogs. (not eating them)
10. Hank also hit a home run in Baltimore. (as well as Felipe)
11. Hank also hit a home run in Baltimore. (as well as in Toronto)
12. Hank also hit a home run in Baltimore. (as well as a foul)
13. He whistled as he walked in the dark, and she was nervous too.
14. She was excited about her speech, and she was nervous too.
15. We didn't try to get out of the cave, but neither did they try to.
16. They didn't get out of the cave, but neither did they try to.
17. Not only is she studying wrestling, she is taking up weight-lifting.
18. Not only is she studying wrestling, she has a professional match.
19. Not only is she studying wrestling, but her roommate is too.
20. Don Quixote just rode Rosinante. (he didn't plow with her)
21. Don Quixote just rode Rosinante. (no other horse)
22. Don Quixote rode just Rosinante.

8.4   Process Adjuncts
(Ref: CGCE 8.19–21)

DIRECTIONS   Underline each **process adjunct,** and indicate whether it denotes either manner (M), or instrument or means (I), by writing the appropriate letter in the blank.

EXAMPLES   They sprayed tear gas <u>indiscriminately</u>.   <u>M</u>

He examined the specimen <u>microscopically</u>.   <u>I</u>

1. He solved the problem automatically.   _____
2. He solved the problem intuitionally. (using intuition)   _____
3. The announcer calmly read the news bulletin.   _____
4. Abercrombie likes to sign his name with a quill pen.   _____
5. He water-skis like an expert.   _____
6. He sorted the coins mechanically. (not paying attention) _____
7. He sorted the coins mechanically. (using a machine)   _____
8. Cassandra took the news philosophically.   _____
9. We are flying BOAC to London.   _____
10. The kitten approached the ball of yarn crab-fashion.   _____
11. The president spoke to the nation on television.   _____
12. The knot was tied the way a sailor might do it.   _____

DIRECTIONS   Use carets to show the places in each sentence where the process adjunct can be added most naturally.

EXAMPLE   Tear gas was ˄ sprayed ˄ .   indiscriminately

13. Pablo plays the cello .   beautifully
14. His signature was forged .   skillfully
15. She could finish the painting sooner .   with a bigger brush
16. She posed for the photographer .   in a fur coat

8.5 Subject Adjuncts

(Ref: CGCE 8.22–23)

DIRECTIONS Underline each **subject adjunct.** Then rephrase the sentence so that the subject adjunct is replaced by an expression more directly related to the subject in its grammar.

EXAMPLE Resentfully, the workers stood by their leaders.

The workers were resentful about standing by their leaders.

1. Regretfully, the council voted to close the park.

   _____

2. The cabbie willingly waited for his passenger.

   _____

3. He had his house painted, reluctantly.

   _____

4. I sincerely invite your questions.

   _____

5. Put your questions in written form, please.

   _____

6. Proudly, the new father told everyone about the twins.

   _____

7. Janette has kindly agreed to sing for us.

   _____

8. I gratefully acknowledge the help of my wife.

   _____

9. Confidently, the salesman began his talk.

   _____

10. Henry sold his Edsel with much regret.

   _____

8.6   Place Adjuncts   (Ref: CGCE 8.24–29)

DIRECTIONS   Underline each **place adjunct,** and indicate whether it is an adjunct of **position** (P) or of **direction** (D) by writing the appropriate letter in the blank.

EXAMPLE   Upstairs the children are running around.   <u>   P   </u>   <u>   D   </u>

1. She stood where the photographer told her.   _____
2. A new building is being constructed nearby.   _____
3. The pickpocket ran that way.   _____
4. The dog jumped into the chair.   _____
5. They met Laura on the library steps.   _____
6. Isadora left her dancing shoes someplace.   _____
7. Here comes Johnny.   _____
8. The house key is inside.   _____
9. She put into the soup everything in the refrigerator.   _____   _____
10. On television, an acrobat is walking over Niagara   _____   _____
    Falls.
11. We drove from the airport past the business district   _____   _____
    to the suburbs.   _____

DIRECTIONS   Use carets and numbers to show the places in each sentence where the place adjuncts can be added most naturally.

EXAMPLE   ^1 The children   are   running ^2 ^1.   1. upstairs   2. around

12.   The shark   swam   quickly .   away

13.   She   grows   whatever she needs   .   in her garden

14.   Herman   brought   a gold medal .   1. back   2. from the Olympics

15.   We   always   eat .   1. on the patio   2. at our house

16.   They're   tossing   a frisbee .   1. back and forth   2. in the park

8.7 Time Adjuncts

(Ref: CGCE 8.30–44)

DIRECTIONS Underline each **time adjunct** and indicate whether it is an adjunct of **time when** (W), **duration** (D), **frequency** (F), or other time expression (X) by writing the appropriate letter in the blank.

EXAMPLE He <u>often</u> arrives <u>at night</u>.   **F**   **W**

1. They are coming from Toronto next week. _____
2. Ted seldom goes to movies. _____
3. Frances is already a CPA. _____
4. Cindy has to leave before midnight. _____
5. They waited while the hamburgers cooked. _____
6. Tomorrow, class will be at nine o'clock. _____ _____
7. Formerly most men worked six days a week. _____ _____
8. Afterwards, they still couldn't play the piccolo. _____ _____
9. We went swimming before breakfast last summer. _____ _____
10. Usually she can chin herself ten times. _____ _____
11. Trollope worked for four hours each morning _____ _____
    when he was writing a book. _____
12. They stayed in Las Vegas a week _____
    after they discovered the slot machines. _____

DIRECTIONS Rewrite the sentences, adding the time adjuncts after each.

13. Lunch lasts.   an hour, often, on Mondays

_____

14. He talked with the dean.   at some length, last year, every term

_____

15. She woke up.   yesterday, in the morning, at two o'clock

_____

8.8   Subclassification of Adjuncts   (Ref: CGCE 8.6–46)

DIRECTIONS   Identify each italicized adjunct as **viewpoint, focusing, intensifier, process, subject, place,** or **time** by writing the appropriate term in the blank.

1. *Historically,* "Richard III" is not a very accurate play.   _____
2. He *just* wants a little butter for his bread.   _____
3. She *strongly* advocates a vegetarian diet.   _____
4. The doorbell rang *insistently.*   _____
5. The porter *purposely* left the door ajar.   _____
6. Our neighbors decided to stay *home.*   _____
7. *Lately,* they have been spending their vacations   _____
   in Bermuda.   _____
8. She *enviously* pretended she didn't care.   _____
9. He opened the olive jar *with a quick twist.*   _____
10. They *clearly* expect to see a flying saucer.   _____
11. We've been waiting *a long while.*   _____
12. They are *mainly* concerned about their grades.   _____
13. *With respect to that problem,* I know nothing.   _____
14. Igor reads music, *too.*   _____

DIRECTIONS   There are other kinds of adjuncts than those illustrated above. What kind of meaning does each italicized adjunct have?

15. He finished the letter in pencil *because he ran out of ink.*

_____

16. He drove fast *so they would get to the theater on time.*

_____

17. She heard the news *from her roommate.*

_____

18. Our mailman was bitten *by a shaggy dog.*

_____

8.9   Questions about Adjuncts   (Ref: CGCE 8.6–46)

DIRECTIONS   For each sentence, write a corresponding question in which an interrogative expression replaces the italicized adjunct.

EXAMPLE   He arrived *last night*.
When did he arrive?
_____

1. The rock concert is *next week*.

   _____

2. The movie lasts *almost four hours*.

   _____

3. It *seldom* rains in the Sahara.

   _____

4. Mr. Matsuya came *from Tokyo*.

   _____

5. Aunt Agatha is living *in a tree house*.

   _____

6. He crossed the Atlantic *on a papyrus raft*.

   _____

7. He dug the hole *with a hoe*.

   _____

8. She made the parachute jump *bravely*.

   _____

9. She likes garlic *quite a lot*.

   _____

10. The show was a success *artistically*.

    _____

11. They stayed home *because of the rain*.

    _____

8.10   Positions of Adjuncts

(Ref: CGCE 8.6–46)

DIRECTIONS   Rewrite each sentence, adding the adjuncts following it. Note the order in which the adjuncts come. More than one arrangement is possible for each sentence; use the one that seems most natural.

1. They made ice cream.   last summer, on their porch, with an electric freezer

_____

2. She is studying Aymara.   at a university in Peru, now

_____

3. He left his umbrella.   in the same place where he had found it, yesterday

_____

4. They watch television.   every Wednesday, for more than an hour, in the evening

_____

5. You see amateurs.   in New York, on the stage, seldom

_____

6. The stream seems to run.   certainly, here, uphill

_____

7. She plays pool.   like an expert, really, sometimes

_____

8. I broke a dish.   carelessly, by dropping it

_____

9. She has a good command of Italian.   conversationally, really

_____

10. He has begun to read *War and Peace*.   only, straight through

_____

11. They feed the alligators.   anymore, never, just

_____

8.11   Adjuncts, Disjuncts, and Conjuncts   (Ref: CGCE 8.2, 4–5)

DIRECTIONS   **Conjuncts** serve to join the clause in which they appear to a preceding clause; they point back to something already said. **Disjuncts** are a loosely connected comment on the form or the content of the rest of the clause; they can often be paraphrased as follows: *Seriously, he left = I am serious in saying that he left.* **Adjuncts** are more closely connected with the rest of the clause: *He talked seriously.* Underline each adverbial, and indicate whether it is an adjunct (A), disjunct (D), or conjunct (C) by writing the appropriate letter in the blank.

1. As for scholarship, Willie is a great success.   _____
2. Angela will consequently be the next astronaut.   _____
3. By comparison, the movie was dull.   _____
4. Confidentially, I hear the governor is resigning.   _____
5. The governor spoke confidentially to the press.   _____
6. George waited until the program ended.   _____
7. He was nevertheless interested.   _____
8. In particular, he reads science fiction.   _____
9. Possibly he is serious.   _____
10. He can't possibly be serious.   _____
11. Otherwise, there is no way to reach Little Rock.   _____
12. Squirrels are hiding nuts in the oak tree.   _____
13. She casually mentioned her election to Phi Beta Kappa.   _____
14. She has rightly decided to seek advice.   _____
15. Some advised her rightly, others wrongly.   _____
16. They don't like cauliflower at all.   _____
17. She married unfortunately. (made a poor choice)   _____
18. She married, unfortunately. (should have stayed single)   _____
19. Will you lend me your book, please?   _____
20. You should write the application in ink.   _____

8.12   Disjuncts

(Ref: CGCE 8.2, 47–52)

DIRECTIONS   Underline each **disjunct**.

1. Honestly, I didn't think Herman would join the army.
2. To be blunt, he is not the intellectual sort.
3. Is it likely, if we can be serious for a moment, that people will buy a three-wheeled car?
4. In your frank opinion, where is the best place to live?
5. Hopefully, the tightrope-walker will walk certainly across the narrow wire.
6. Certainly, the explorer will be looking hopefully for the lost city.
7. Nobody is perfect, of course.
8. The river is receding, which is lucky.

DIRECTIONS   Underline the disjuncts; then paraphrase each sentence so that the disjunct in it is replaced by a complement or verb element.

EXAMPLES   Obviously, nobody expected us to be here.

It is obvious that nobody expected us to be here.

They arrived, to our surprise, before we did.

It surprised us that they arrived before we did.

9. A burnt child naturally dreads the fire.

_____

10. To his amazement, somebody moved into the haunted house.

_____

11. He foolishly left the keys in his car.

_____

12. Admittedly we have too many pets.

_____

8.13   Conjuncts

(Ref: CGCE 8.2, 53–56)

DIRECTIONS   Underline each **conjunct.**

1. Next, Louella decided to run for mayor.
2. What is more, she is likely to be elected.
3. We suspect, by the way, that Theodosia will run too.
4. So the race should be an interesting one.
5. We can expect, for example, some dirty tricks.
6. At any rate, they are both qualified for the office.
7. This will be, moreover, an important election.
8. Meanwhile back at the ranch Dale was waiting for Roy.
9. On the other hand, the jury may be hung.

DIRECTIONS   To the second clause in each set, add an appropriate conjunct.

EXAMPLE   It was a difficult test. _▲ **Nevertheless** He made an A on it.

10. If the plane from Chicago is late, we can make our connection.

11. The team won every game, and the fans supported them.

12. You ought to wait a bit longer, or you will miss the fireworks.

13. Lee wore a red wig. Nobody noticed him.

14. At first Arizona seemed hot. We got used to it.

15. She is an ailurophobe. She hates cats.

16. We didn't follow them. They followed us.

● 9.1 Ellipsis

(Ref: CGCE 9.1–6)

DIRECTIONS What part of each sentence might be omitted as an **ellipsis**? Put parentheses around the words to be omitted.

EXAMPLE She might sing, but I don't think she will (sing.)

1. The doorbell was ringing, and the phone was ringing too.
2. Jill was falling down the hill while Jack was falling down the hill.
3. When they are frozen, bananas will keep indefinitely.
4. The bus that was scheduled to take us to the field broke down.
5. Postage stamps are intended to be used, or else postage stamps are intended to be collected.
6. If he was nervous while he was giving his speech, he didn't appear to be nervous.

DIRECTIONS Rewrite the sentences, supplying the omitted material.

EXAMPLE Beg your pardon. **I beg your pardon.** _____

7. Seen any good movies lately?

_____

8. See you tomorrow.

_____

9. Anyone home?

_____

10. Nice to meet you.

_____

11. They ready yet?

_____

9.2 Coordination and Subordination (Ref: CGCE 9.7–15)

DIRECTIONS In **coordination,** the items are grammatically of equal function. **Syndetic coordination** uses a **coordinator** (coordinating conjunction); **asyndetic coordination** does not. In **subordination,** on the other hand, one item is dependent on the other. Are the italicized expressions examples of syndetic coordination (SC), asyndetic coordination (AC), or subordination (S)? Write the appropriate abbreviation in the blank.

1. He jumped *out of the frying pan and into the fire.* _____

2. Al plays the drum *all day, all night.* _____

3. He gives drum lessons *in the living room of his apartment.* _____

4. The quarterback is *ready, willing, eager* to play. _____

5. The blue-plate special is *ready and good.* _____

6. The donkey won't move until it is *good and ready.* _____

7. She plays *tennis, golf, softball*—you name it. _____

8. *Bob and Carol and Ted and Alice* will be here soon. _____

9. *I came, I saw, I conquered.* _____

10. *After I saw what was going on, I put a stop to it.* _____

DIRECTIONS Indicate whether the clauses in each sentence are joined by a **subordinating conjunction** (SC), a **coordinating conjunction** (CC), or a **conjunct** (C). Write the appropriate abbreviation in the blank.

11. Her plants grow, because she talks to them. _____

12. She talks to her plants, so they grow. _____

13. She talks to her plants, and they grow. _____

14. He likes Bach, but she prefers rock. _____

15. He likes Bach, although she prefers rock. _____

16. He likes Bach; however, she prefers rock. _____

17. He is going bowling, or he would be at the meeting. _____

18. He is going bowling; otherwise he would be at the meeting. _____

19. He would be at the meeting, if he weren't going bowling. _____

9.3   Semantic Implications of Coordinators   (Ref: CGCE 9.16–18)

DIRECTIONS   The meaning of a coordinating conjunction can often be made more explicit by an adverbial; some examples are—

and: also, likewise, similarly; then (if . . . then); then, thereafter; therefore; rather, in contrast; nevertheless, still

  or: also, too, or both; else, instead; in other words

but: rather, on the contrary; yet, nevertheless

Indicate the semantic implication of the coordination in these sentences by adding an adverbial or otherwise rephrasing.

1. Hezekiah was illiterate, but he made a fortune on the stock market.

   _____

2. Sarah did not buy vegetables at the market, but grew them herself.

   _____

3. We are taking a vacation in the mountains, or we're going to the seashore.

   _____

4. Do you want sugar in your coffee, or do you want cream?

   _____

5. He was a funambulist, or a tightrope-walker.

   _____

6. Alf's car broke down, and he had to walk to a garage.

   _____

7. She read *Tom Jones,* and she wrote an essay on it.

   _____

8. Come over to my place, and we can study together.

   _____

9. Rhoda is taking Latin, and she is studying Greek.

   _____

10. The railroad is bankrupt, and it is running.

   _____

11. She is studying law, and her brother is a beach bum.

   _____

9.4 Correlatives; Adverbial Focus (Ref: CGCE 9.19–20, 27)

DIRECTIONS **Correlative expressions** sometimes join clauses:

both . . . and
either . . . or
neither . . . nor
not . . . neither/nor
not . . . but rather
not only . . . but also

Combine each pair of clauses by means of the most appropriate correlative expression.

1. He will go to summer school. He will spend the summer in Europe.

   _____

2. She has not driven a truck. He has not ridden on a motorcycle.

   _____

3. He is not vacationing in Florida. He is working there.

   _____

4. Thieves broke into the house. They ransacked it.

   _____

5. She wears a nose jewel. She has pierced ears.

   _____

6. Whales are not fish. Porpoises are not either.

   _____

DIRECTIONS Indicate the scope of the italicized adverbial by putting parentheses around the part of the sentence to which it applies.

7. *At noon,* the bells ring and the sirens go off.
8. The bells won't ring, but the sirens go off *at noon.*
9. Pat is *certainly* working hard, but Mike is loafing.
10. Pat is working hard, *certainly,* but Mike is loafing.
11. Pat is working hard and Mike is loafing, *certainly.*
12. Pat is working hard, but Mike is *certainly* loafing.

9.5   Ellipsis in Coordinated Clauses   (Ref: CGCE 9.21–30)

DIRECTIONS   Combine each pair of sentences with a coordinating conjunction and omit as much identical material as possible.

EXAMPLE   Peter ate a cheese sandwich. Peter drank a glass of beer.

Peter ate a cheese sandwich and drank a glass of beer.

1. Willie came to bat. Willie hit a homer.

2. TV has been changing. TV has not been improving.

3. John will stay home. Mary will go to work.

4. He sent his congressman a letter. He sent his senator a telegram.

5. Tom flew the plane to Chicago. Sue flew the plane to Omaha.

6. We have moved already. They will move soon.

7. The show may be held over. The show probably will be held over.

8. The demonstration has already started. The demonstration will start soon.

9. Perry asked the question seriously. Paul answered the question seriously.

10. We can go to the first show. We can go to the last show.

11. Today Margaret challenged Billie Jean. Today Billie Jean defeated her.

9.6   Phrasal Coordination

(Ref: CGCE 9.31–39)

DIRECTIONS   Replace the **conjoined clauses** by a single clause with a **conjoined phrase.** Be prepared to indicate what kind of item has been conjoined in each case.

1. The streets were covered with ice, and the sidewalks were covered with ice.

   _____

2. This coat will fit tall men, or it will fit short men.

   _____

3. She didn't believe this explanation; she didn't believe that explanation.

   _____

4. There are many small mammals that swim, and there are many small reptiles that swim.

   _____

5. He reads in bed, and he reads at the table, and he reads on the bus.

   _____

6. She travels to Montreal, and she travels from Montreal.

   _____

7. She went to Montreal, or she went to Quebec.

   _____

8. Cross the street after you stop; cross the street after you look.

   _____

9. They photographed him before he shaved, and they photographed him after he shaved.

   _____

10. He was certain to try, or at least he was likely to try.

   _____

9.7   Order in Coordination   (Ref: CGCE 9.40)

DIRECTIONS   In what order do the following **conjoins** appear when they are coordinated? Write the coordination for each.

1. eggs, ham _____   10. pepper, salt   _____
2. ink, pen   _____   11. men, women   _____
3. old, young _____   12. gentlemen, ladies _____
4. left, right _____   13. head, shoulders _____
5. feet, hands _____   14. easy, free   _____
6. ears, eyes _____   15. bacon, eggs   _____
7. bad, good _____   16. husband, wife _____
8. jump, run _____   17. fingers, toes _____
9. cap, gown _____   18. needle, thread _____

DIRECTIONS   A difference of order in a conjunction may imply a difference of meaning. What is the implied difference of meaning in the following pairs?

19. a. He answered the phone and talked loudly.

    b. He talked loudly and answered the phone.

    _____

20. a. He carried the garbage through the kitchen door and across the yard.

    b. He carried the garbage across the yard and through the kitchen door.

    _____

21. a. Let's see the movie and go.

    b. Let's go and see the movie.

    _____

22. a. He slammed the window shut, and the cat let out a yowl.

    b. The cat let out a yowl, and he slammed the window shut.

    _____

23. a. Willie hit another home run and tied the game.

    b. Willie tied the game and hit another home run.

    _____

9.8 Segregatory and Combinatory Coordination (Ref: CGCE 9.41–42)

DIRECTIONS In **segregatory coordination,** what is said applies to each conjoin, independently of the other. In **combinatory coordination,** the conjoins must be taken together for the meaning of the sentence to be appropriate. In the most probable interpretation of each sentence, is the coordination segregatory (S) or combinatory (C)? Write the appropriate letter in the blank.

EXAMPLES   John and Mary have a cold.   **S**

John and Mary make a nice couple.   **C**

1. The solid-colored ties are red and black. _____
2. The striped ties are red and black. _____
3. Romeo and Juliet were married. _____
4. Romeo and Benedict were married. _____
5. Damon and Pythias are good friends. _____
6. Hector and Achilles are good fighters. _____
7. Ted and Alice were both winners. _____
8. Ted and Alice were the winner. _____
9. He spent most of his life in Minneapolis and St. Paul. _____
10. He spent parts of his life in Pasadena and New Rochelle. _____
11. Mary and Rhoda ate a watermelon each. _____
12. Mary and Rhoda ate a watermelon together. _____
13. Does he drink too much and sing a lot? _____
14. Does he eat a lot and drink too much? _____
15. They went to Paris by ship and by train. _____
16. They went to Hong Kong and Edinburgh by ship and by train, respectively. _____
17. Bob and Carol play bridge with Ted and Alice. _____
18. Bob and Carol were the respective partners of Ted and Alice. _____

9.9 Identical Items; Quasi-Coordinators   (Ref: CGCE 9.43–44)

DIRECTIONS   Rewrite to express the meaning of the coordinated identical items in some other way.

1. He is growing taller and taller every year.

   _____

2. They keep moving farther and farther away.

   _____

3. They ran and ran and ran until they were exhausted.

   _____

4. The rocket shot up and up.

   _____

5. The shop has bòoks and bòoks and bòoks.

   _____

6. There are jókes and jòkes.

   _____

DIRECTIONS   Replace the quasi-coordinators with true coordinators, making any other necessary changes.

7. Joseph, with his eleven brothers, is at the well.

   _____

8. Aeneas, as well as Ulysses, has a long sea voyage before him.

   _____

9. Bridge more than golf is his hobby.

   _____

10. He is curious as much as interested.

   _____

11. She worked hopefully rather than confidently on the problem.

   _____

12. She patted in addition to spanking the dog.

   _____

9.10   Ambiguity in Coordination   (Ref: CGCE 9.1–44)

DIRECTIONS   Each of the following sentences has an ambiguous coordination or ellipsis. Rephrase each sentence in two ways to make the ambiguous meanings clear.

1. Henry visited Jill on Monday and Hank on Tuesday.

2. Tokyo is bigger than New York, and London too.

3. Dian has appeared in two or three movies.

4. Only athletic women and men play football.

DIRECTIONS   A coordinate phrase sometimes has a different meaning from the corresponding coordinate clauses. Describe the probable difference of meaning in the following pairs.

5. a. Will the defendant testify and be acquitted?
   b. Will the defendant testify, and will he be acquitted?

6. a. Did he either fly or sáil to Europe?
   b. Did he flý, or did he sàil to Europe?

7. a. He reads important and entertaining books.
   b. He reads important books, and he reads entertaining books.

9.11   Apposition (1)   (Ref: CGCE 9.45–58)

DIRECTIONS   Put parentheses around each structure of **apposition** and divide the two parts with a slash. Some **appositives** have other appositives inside them.

EXAMPLES   **(**A neighbor,/Fred Brick,**)** is on the telephone.

(The symbol,/**(**a letter/*x*,**))**was painted in red.

1. The biggest country in the Western Hemisphere, Brazil, is populated mainly on the coast.

2. Brazil, the biggest country in the Western Hemisphere, is populated mainly on the coast.

3. His hobby, collecting wine bottles, takes a lot of space.

4. The play, a comedy of Shakespeare's, has closed.

5. The fact that Donald was wrong didn't bother him.

6. The dogs, each with his tail between his legs, crept in.

7. The question of when to leave never came up.

8. A woman, Socrates' wife, Xanthippe, emptied a pot on his head.

9. The Russian word *troika* 'vehicle drawn by three horses' has been borrowed into English.

10. The singer, a countertenor (i.e., male alto), was applauded.

DIRECTIONS   Some appositives have indicators of the semantic relationship between them. Underline the indicators in the following.

11. She was a chiromancer, in other words, a palm-reader.

12. Many languages have no articles—for instance, Russian and Latin.

13. She is sensitive to stings, mainly those of wasps.

14. He announced his intention of running for office.

15. Mt. Everest, or Chomolungma, is the world's tallest mountain.

9.12   Apposition (2)   (Ref: CGCE 9.45–58)

DIRECTIONS   Combine the sentences by inserting the second as an appositive into the first.

1. The first president wore false teeth. He was George Washington.

_____

2. Alaska is the largest state. It is the newest state in the union.

_____

3. An Indian came down from the hills. He was the last of his tribe.

_____

4. He wears a yarmulka. A yarmulka is a skull cap.

5. Two answers were on the card. Both answers were wrong.

_____

6. Some holidays always fall on Monday. An example is Labor Day.

_____

7. They enjoy card games. They particularly enjoy cribbage.

_____

8. The word has two pronunciations. The word referred to is *either.*

_____

9. My son is visiting me. That son is the one who is the doctor.

_____

10. Jones had a press conference. Jones has the position of president.

_____

11. He didn't like the suggestion. It was that he join the army.

_____

12. Their decision was a wise one. They decided to leave.

_____

9.13 Apposition—Restrictive   (Ref: CGCE 9.46, 56–58)
and Nonrestrictive

DIRECTIONS   Punctuate, by placing commas around any **nonrestrictive appositives.**
Leave **restrictive appositives** unpunctuated.

EXAMPLES   A lawyer ⌄ Mr. Campbell ⌄ was here last night.

The famous lawyer John Campbell was here last night.

1. She is watching a movie with her favorite actor Paul Newman.
2. Actor Paul Newman is also known as a director.
3. I forgot how to spell a word *accommodate.*
4. I can never remember whether the verb *lose* has one *o* or two.
5. Gregory the Great is the most famous churchman of that name.
6. Augustine a theologian from Africa wrote the *Confessions.*
7. Many know Hillel's saying "If not now, when?"
8. He has an idea that the earth is shrinking.
9. He had only one ambition that he would open a pizza stand.

DIRECTIONS   Put parentheses around the terms that are in restrictive apposition, and
separate the two parts with a slash.

EXAMPLE   (That famous critic/Paul Jones) is lecturing today.

10. The movie *Fanny Hill* was quite different from the novel.
11. My uncle George has just gone to Zanzibar.
12. Yeats the poet is better known than Yeats the playwright.
13. We spent the summer with Cousin Bette.
14. Pianist Liberace and band-leader Mick Jagger have teamed up.
15. He rejected the suggestion that he should resign.
16. She considered the problem of whether to stay or not.
17. He had an opportunity to live on a kibbutz.

9.14   Nonrestrictive Apposition

(Ref: CGCE 9.49–55)

DIRECTIONS   The appositives in a nonrestrictive apposition can have various semantic relationships between them. By writing the appropriate symbol in the blank, indicate which of the following relationships each apposition involves:

> appellation (Ap)
> designation (D)
> identification (I)
> reformulation (R)
> attribution (At)
> exemplification (E)
> particularization (P)

1. The first-prize winner, Ermengard Jones, was disqualified.   _____

2. Ermengard Jones, the first-prize winner, was disqualified.   _____

3. There is a rumor going around—that classes will be canceled.   _____

4. It is a sitcom (situation comedy) show.   _____

5. Gypsy Rose Lee, a well-known author, was also an ecdysiast.   _____

6. Most of the Presidents—Madison, Lincoln, Garfield, etc.—have lived in the White House.   _____

7. They like Mexican food, particularly enchiladas.   _____

8. The Romans, especially those of the later Empire, developed a vast bureaucracy.   _____

9. Norse mythology envisioned the universe as a cosmic tree, by name, Yggdrasil.   _____

10. It is a quadrilateral, more precisely, a parallelogram.   _____

11. She is related to a bandit, Jesse James, in fact.   _____

12. Anne, the last of the Stuarts to reign, had no surviving children.   _____

13. In folk tales, the youngest son, clearly the best of the lot, always succeeds.   _____

14. The vowels, such as *a* and *u*, are more sonorous than the consonants.   _____

● **10.1   Factors in Sentence Connection**   (Ref: CGCE 10.1–4)

DIRECTIONS   Read the paragraph and answer the following questions about its sentence connections.

[1] Keimer wore his beard at full length, because somewhere in the Mosaic law it is said, "Thou shalt not mar the corners of thy beard." [2] He likewise kept the seventh day, Sabbath; [3] and these two points were essentials with him. [4] I disliked both, but agreed to admit them upon the condition of his adopting the doctrine of using no animal food. [5] "I doubt," said he, "my constitution will not bear that." [6] I assured him it would and that he would be the better for it. [7] He was usually a great glutton, [8] and I promised myself some diversion in half starving him. [9] He agreed to try the practice, if I would keep him company. [10] I did so, [11] and we held it for three months. . . . [12] I went on pleasantly, [13] but poor Keimer suffered grievously, tired of the project, longed for the fleshpots of Egypt, and ordered a roast pig. [14] He invited me and two women friends to dine with him; [15] but, it being brought too soon upon table, he could not resist the temptation, and ate the whole before we came.

—BENJAMIN FRANKLIN, from *The Autobiography*

1. What words in [2] link that sentence to [1]? _____
2. What phrase in [3] links it to [1] and [2]? _____
3. What word in [5] links it to [4]? _____
4. To what sentence does the first *it* in [6] refer? _____
5. To what sentence does the second *it* in [6] refer? _____
6. What two words contrast semantically in [7] and [8]? _____
7. What phrase in [9] links it to [4]? _____
8. *So* in [10] replaces what phrase in [9]? _____
9. What adverbial could be added in [11] to make the meaning of *and* clearer? _____
10. What signals the contrast of meaning in [12] and [13]? _____
11. *Dine* in [14] is semantically connected with what phrase in [13]? _____
_____
12. A *roast pig* in [13] is echoed once by substitution and twice by ellipsis in [15]. What is the substitute for it? _____
13. Point out some other devices by which the sentences in this paragraph are linked. _____
_____

10.2   Time and Place Relaters   (Ref: CGCE 10.5–8)

DIRECTIONS   Underline the expressions of time and place that serve to connect sentences.

1. Sylvester Graham advocated the use of whole-wheat flour. The graham cracker was later named after him.

2. In 1877 Edison invented the phonograph. His next invention was the electric light.

3. The Wright brothers began modern aviation. Human flight had already been studied by men like Leonardo da Vinci.

4. The Shasta daisy was developed by Luther Burbank. An earlier discovery was the Burbank potato.

5. Alexander Graham Bell trained teachers of the deaf. At the same time, he was developing the telephone.

6. The White House was designed by James Hoban. John Adams was the first president to live there.

7. Chaucer's tomb in Westminster Abbey is the nucleus of Poets' Corner. Many other writers are buried nearby.

8. The Indians did a vigorous rain dance for the tourists. Shortly thereafter, there was a cloudburst.

9. The great ocean liner steamed majestically out of the port toward the open sea. A gaggle of tugboats followed.

10. The mayor's house is a three-story brick structure in Georgian style. The adjacent buildings are wooden.

11. A large crowd dressed in odd costumes filled the auditorium. A couple of chickens sat in front.

12. A long, black limousine with much chrome dominated the lot. A small, beat-up coupe was parked opposite.

10.3   Logical Connecters

(Ref: CGCE 10.9–24)

DIRECTIONS   Supply a **logical connecter** that might be used to link the sentences in each group.

1. Alexander Melville Bell invented a phonetic alphabet. His son invented the telephone.   _____

2. Although he wrote six hundred years ago, Chaucer is still widely read for a number of reasons. He is a link _____ between the Middle Ages and the Renaissance. He was _____ admired and imitated by subsequent authors. He _____ writes about situations and people that are like those of our own time. He is entertaining to read.   _____

3. Soybeans are easy to grow, and they are nutritious. There are many ways they can be prepared as food.   _____

4. Thomas does not believe in astrology. He does not believe in numerology.   _____

5. English spelling is inconsistent, unpredictable, archaic, and hard to learn. It is a nuisance.   _____

6. The metric system is easier than the traditional English measures and is far more widely used. The United States is adopting it.   _____

7. Willie has had difficulty in relating to his peers constructively. He beats up his classmates.   _____

8. The Russian alphabet has some letters that are different from ours. And the Arabic script is entirely different. The hardest writing system for us to learn is Chinese.   _____

9. Alice is not going to join a commune. She has decided to be a hermit.   _____

10. Ice hockey is a dangerous sport. A good many people play it.   _____

11. They say chess is hard to learn. It is rather easy.   _____

12. The Romans adopted Hellenic religion, Hellenic theater, and Hellenic philosophy. They greatly admired Greek culture.   _____

10.4 Substitution and Ellipsis

(Ref: CGCE 10.25–29)

DIRECTIONS Rewrite the second sentence in each pair, substituting pro-forms for the repeated elements or omitting them.

1. Mr. and Mrs. Jones went to see the lawyer. Mr. and Mrs. Jones wanted the lawyer to draw up a will.

   _____

2. The players have dressed out for the game. The players' coach is urging the players to win the game.

   _____

3. There are two movies that Yolanda wants to see. Yolanda will go to the nearest movie.

   _____

4. One movie is French. The other movie is Italian, but both of the movies have subtitles.

   _____

5. They wanted to have the meeting on Monday at the city hall. The city hall is a good place for the meeting, but there are no rooms available on Monday.

   _____

6. You and I can study at the library. You and I are sure to find a quiet place at the library.

   _____

7. I like to get mail. Most people like to get mail.

   _____

8. —Are you and Alice going to the rally tonight? —No, Alice and I are not going to the rally tonight.

   _____

9. Geraldine will play the leading role. At least, I think Geraldine will play the leading role.

   _____

10. The team is training hard. They need to train hard.

   _____

10.5   Complex Pro-Forms   (Ref: CGCE 10.30–36)

DIRECTIONS   For each of the sentences, write a response following the pattern indicated.

EXAMPLE   John drives a car (*so* + auxiliary + subject)

So does Bob. _____

1. Ollie has been to Tijuana. (*so* + auxiliary + subject)

   _____

2. I am riding with no hands. (*so* + subject + auxiliary)

   _____

3. Will you return the book soon? (subject + auxiliary + *do* + *so*)

   _____

4. He should lock up. (subject + auxiliary + *do* + *that*)

   _____

5. The girls want to wash your car. (subject + auxiliary + *do* + *it*)

   _____

6. Poor Albert looks sunburned. (subject + auxiliary)

   _____

7. Moe lost his surfboard at the beach. (auxiliary + subject + *do* + *that?*)

   _____

8. Somebody needs to turn the phonograph off. (subject + *do* + *it!*)

   _____

9. Ted likes to cook. (*not* + subject)

   _____

10. Sally won't drive. (*neither* + auxiliary + subject)

   _____

10.6 Discourse Reference

(Ref: CGCE 10.37–42)

DIRECTIONS   Underline the expression that has **deictic reference,** and put parentheses around the words to which it refers. Indicate whether the reference is **anaphoric** (pointing backward) or **cataphoric** (pointing forward).

EXAMPLES   <u>Here</u> is the news. **(**A diplomat was kidnapped last night

in London.**)**   cataphoric

They regularly take **(**the *Daily Courier***)**. I wouldn't

read <u>a paper like that</u>.   anaphoric

1. This is the best way to learn Russian: Spend a year or two in Russia.   _____

2. Steve plays his hi-fi at top volume while he works. This bothers his roommate.   _____

3. They wanted to push the old car over the edge of a cliff. But that is against the law.   _____

4. *Moby Dick* begins thus: "Call me Ishmael. Some years ago . . ."   _____

5. He plays real New Orleans jazz. That is an older form than the Chicago style.   _____

6. He wore sandals and a tank top. Someone said there was a rule against the latter.   _____

7. The airplane was very large, with a huge tail but almost no wings. I have never before now seen such a plane.   _____

8. It amazed everyone in the planetarium. The roof of the building looked exactly like the night sky.   _____

9. There was a late freeze and there were prolonged droughts. Such were the causes of this year's grain shortage.   _____

10. A chimpanzee may use a stick to force termites out of their nest. The foregoing is an example of tool use by animals.   _____

10.7   Ellipsis in Dialog

(Ref: CGCE 10.43–47)

DIRECTIONS   Expand the ellipsis in the second sentence of each dialog.

EXAMPLE   —Have you spoken to the doctor? —Yes, I have.
Yes, I have spoken to him.   *or*   **Yes, I have done so.**

1. —Many people have sailed around the world. —But Magellan was the first.

2. —Will man ever land on Mars? —Very likely.

3. —They're making a musical out of *War and Peace*. —How?

4. —The holidays begin next Wednesday. —Maybe sooner.

5. —Do you think Sam will win the tourney? —No one but.

6. —Would you like to join us for lunch? —At noon?

7. —As an appetizer they served jelly fish. —Jelly fish?

8. —They are crossing the Atlantic in a Norwegian ship. —The plane is faster.

9. —Which is older, the harpsichord or the clavichord? —The clavichord, I think.

10. —It is likely to rain. —I hope not.

10.8   Structural Parallelism   (Ref: CGCE 10.48)

DIRECTIONS   Point out which sentences of the following paragraphs are connected by structural parallelism. The sentences have been numbered for ease of reference.

[1] In your hands, my fellow citizens, more than mine, will rest the final success or failure of our course. [2] Since this country was founded, each generation of Americans has been summoned to give testimony to its national loyalty. [3] The graves of young Americans who answered the call to service surround the globe. [4] Now the trumpet summons us again—not as a call to bear arms, though arms we need—not as a call to battle, though embattled we are—but a call to bear the burden of a long twilight struggle, year in and year out, "rejoicing in hope, patient in tribulation"—a struggle against the common enemies of man: tyranny, poverty, disease and war itself.

[5] Can we forge against these enemies a grand and global alliance, North and South, East and West, that can assure a more fruitful life for all mankind? [6] Will you join in that historic effort?

[7] In the long history of the world, only a few generations have been granted the role of defending freedom in its hour of maximum danger. [8] I do not shrink from this responsibility—[9] I welcome it. [10] I do not believe that any of us would exchange places with any other people or any other generation. [11] The energy, the faith, the devotion which we bring to this endeavor will light our country and all who serve it—[12] and the glow from that fire can truly light the world.

[13] And so, my fellow Americans: ask not what your country can do for you—[14] ask what you can do for your country.

[15] My fellow citizens of the world: ask not what America will do for you, but what together we can do for the freedom of man.

[16] Finally, whether you are citizens of America or citizens of the world, ask of us here the same high standards of strength and sacrifice which we ask of you. [17] With a good conscience our only sure reward, with history the final judge of our deeds, let us go forth to lead the land we love, but knowing that here on earth God's work must truly be our own.

—JOHN FITZGERALD KENNEDY, from the Inaugural Address

● 11.1 Coordination and Subordination   (Ref: CGCE 11.1)

DIRECTIONS Which sentences are **complex**, that is, contain a **subordinate clause** (S), and which are **compound**, that is, contain **coordinate clauses** (C)? Write the appropriate letter in the blank.

1. The light turned green, and the traffic began to move.   _____

2. After the light turned green, the traffic began to move.   _____

3. I think that the golf pro is giving a lesson.   _____

4. The golf pro is giving a lesson, or at least I think so.   _____

5. She went to the beach so she could get a suntan.   _____

6. She went to the beach, and so she got a suntan.   _____

7. There was a solar eclipse, but the sky was overcast.   _____

8. There was a solar eclipse, although the sky was overcast.   _____

DIRECTIONS Put parentheses around each subordinate clause, including any that is embedded in another subordinate clause.

EXAMPLE I think (that you can do it (if you try.))

9. While the boar was roasting in a covered pit, everyone danced the hula.

10. He asked whether anyone had found his car keys.

11. It is important that there should be warning lights at every railroad crossing.

12. As she was wondering when the elevator would come, she noticed the out-of-order sign.

13. I expect the parade will start as soon as the rain stops.

14. Because the house was empty, some thought it was haunted.

15. He decided he would live in a castle after he visited one on the Rhine.

11.2 Finite, Nonfinite, and Verbless Clauses (Ref: CGCE 11.2–5)

DIRECTIONS Is each italicized clause **finite** (F), **nonfinite** (N), or **verbless** (V)? Write the appropriate letter in the blank.

EXAMPLES *Because John is working,* he is not here. **F**

Having seen the pictures, he left the gallery. **N**

John, *then in New York,* was working for the UN. **V**

1. The people *living outside the city* are being annexed. _____
2. *Alice having started the fire,* Bess put it out. _____
3. *If he ordered the pizza,* he must have a big appetite. _____
4. You should not drink very cold water *while hot from work.* _____
5. *Standing on her head* makes Yolanda dizzy. _____
6. You can't do that, *whether on the roller coaster or not.* _____
7. It is necessary *for everyone to sit in a circle.* _____
8. *A letter home finally written,* Theo went to supper. _____
9. *When the floor is polished,* it looks like marble. _____
10. *Tossed out of windows all along the parade route,* confetti littered the streets. _____
11. You should wear seat belts *while you are riding.* _____
12. He wanted *to design a new sort of skyscraper.* _____
13. *With the moon in its waxing phase,* it is hard to observe the stars. _____
14. I can't imagine *why the bell is ringing.* _____
15. She talks about her friends, *all of them television stars.* _____
16. We heard *Sammy sing at the Hollywood Bowl.* _____
17. *Although they open the door at noon,* you can get in earlier. _____
18. The nursemaid strolled in the park, *two babies with her.* _____

11.3 Formal Indicators of Subordination (Ref: CGCE 11.6–9)

DIRECTIONS Circle the **indicator of subordination** in each sentence.

EXAMPLE The dew will evaporate (after) the sun rises.

1. They waited until the crowd left.
2. The dog was digging where the bone was buried.
3. The auctioneer studied in order to learn his trade.
4. Now that winter is here, spring cannot be far behind.
5. As long as you are up, will you get me a glass?
6. He would call a taxi rather than walk a block.
7. In case one clock stops, there is another in the front room.
8. Johnson knows why they are late.
9. Marla wondered whether she was lost.
10. It was lucky that the door was unlocked.

DIRECTIONS Combine the two clauses in each group by inserting the second into the first as a subordinate clause, with some indicator of subordination. Circle the indicator of subordination in the new sentence.

EXAMPLE We met her. We were leaving the room.

We met her (as) we were leaving the room. _____

11. They took their seats. The play was half over.

_____

12. We should stop. The traffic policeman signaled.

_____

13. We were glad. The electricity came back on.

_____

14. The receptionist told him. The doctor would see him soon.

_____

15. They found the bone. A dog had been digging there.

_____

11.4 Functions of Subordinate Clauses (Ref: CGCE 11.10–12)

DIRECTIONS Put parentheses around each subordinate clause and identify its function as one of the following by writing the appropriate abbreviation in the blank:

S	subject	Pm	postmodifier in a noun phrase
Od	direct object	Cp	complement of a preposition
Oi	indirect object	Ca	complement of an adjective
Cs	subject complement	Aj	adjunct
Co	object complement	Dj	disjunct
Ap	appositive	Cj	conjunct

1. How the squirrel got into the attic is a mystery. _____
2. Everyone is glad that the Maple Leafs are playing. _____
3. Willie still doesn't believe that the earth is round. _____
4. He ran back to where he had started. _____
5. Their orders are that they are to march to the river. _____
6. The waiter who took our order has disappeared. _____
7. The mariner told whomever he met the same story. _____
8. And, what is just as important, she swims the butterfly. _____
9. She found it what she expected. _____
10. If I may say so, golf is less interesting than tennis. _____
11. The idea that space is curved was suggested by Einstein. _____
12. The idea that came to him in his sleep was an inspiration. _____
13. The train started after the conductor signaled. _____
14. Her question, whether the dorms are coed, surprised them. _____
15. The movie was what we expected. _____
16. Morris asked when the paper was due. _____
17. That the butler committed the murder is a cliché. _____
18. Mission Control is anxious lest the astronauts run short of fuel. _____
19. We wondered about how Plymouth Plantation got started. _____
20. He can make himself whatever he wants. _____

11.5   Nominal Clauses

(Ref: CGCE 11.13–19)

DIRECTIONS   Put parentheses around each **nominal clause,** and indicate what structural type it is and what function it has, using the following numbers and abbreviations:

STRUCTURAL
TYPES

1. *that*-clause
2. *wh*- interrogative
3. *yes-no* interrogative
4. nominal relative

5. *to*-infinitive nominal
6. bare infinitive
7. nominal *-ing*
8. verbless clause

FUNCTIONS

S   subject
Od   direct object
Oi   indirect object
Ap   appositive

Cs   subject complement
Co   object complement
Cp   complement of preposition
Ca   complement of adjective

	TYPE	FUNCTION
1. The fact that he ate a cup of cement may account for his stomachache.	_____	_____
2. We thought the butler did it.	_____	_____
3. Ten people in one VW makes a crowded ride.	_____	_____
4. The question is which book to read.	_____	_____
5. She asked when he was last on a merry-go-round.	_____	_____
6. Whether the movie is in color or not is no matter.	_____	_____
7. Nobody knows if today is a postal holiday.	_____	_____
8. They give whoever asks them the same answer.	_____	_____
9. For Phineas to go bird-watching is quite unusual.	_____	_____
10. He was eager to hold the door open.	_____	_____
11. The engineers were afraid of the dam breaking.	_____	_____
12. The judge's denying the motion came as no surprise.	_____	_____
13. They named the boy what his grandfather suggested.	_____	_____
14. She earns money by mowing lawns.	_____	_____
15. The best thing is take a lot of notes.	_____	_____

11.6   Adverbial Clauses   (Ref: CGCE 11.20–34)

DIRECTIONS   Put parentheses around each **adverbial clause** and underline its **subordinator.**

EXAMPLE   (<u>When</u> I last saw you,) you lived in Washington.

1. The theater was empty when the movie started.
2. After spending a week in Luxembourg, they went to Liechtenstein.
3. He never drives while under the influence of alcohol.
4. Answer the questions, wherever applicable.
5. There is now a thirty-story hotel where we used to picnic.
6. If the car won't start, we'll have to walk.
7. We'll have to walk, unless the car starts.
8. Although she slipped once, Olga was the best on the balance beam.
9. Whether or not the game is telecast, we are going to see it live.
10. Whatever you ask for, they serve ketchup and mustard.
11. Phineas shaved all his hair off because he wanted to be cool.
12. Inasmuch as all aspirin is the same formula, we buy the cheapest.
13. In order to get a good seat, you have to get to the stadium early.
14. She changed her hair style and wore dark glasses, so that no one recognized her.
15. He delivered the speech just as he had practiced it.
16. He waited hours for a ticket rather than miss the opening game.
17. The more the audience laughed, the funnier the comedian became.
18. As bees love nectar, men love flattery.
19. Seeing that it is already 5:00, the store is probably closed.
20. No matter how often I learn the Greek alphabet, I forget it.

11.7   Subordinating Conjunctions   (Ref: CGCE 11.20–34)

DIRECTIONS   Rewrite the italicized clauses, adding a **subordinator** to each.

EXAMPLE   *Nearing the entrance,* I shook hands with my friends.
As I neared the entrance,   *or*   **While nearing the entrance,**
_____

1. The dog, *having crossed the road,* ran up to the mailman.
_____

2. *Were there time,* we would be glad to wait for you.
_____

3. *Being eager to leave,* she stood at the door and put on her coat.
_____

4. *The city being very crowded,* he likes to spend weekends in the country.
_____

5. She got up at four in the morning *to see the satellite.*
_____

6. *The game having ended,* the streets were suddenly crowded.
_____

7. Sadie opened the mail box but, *looking in,* saw nothing.
_____

8. *Had you told us what you wanted,* we could have helped you.
_____

9. It takes either skill or luck *to win with a bridge hand like that.*
_____

10. *Say what you will,* Murray is going to hike to Alaska.
_____

11.8   Dangling Clauses   (Ref: CGCE 11.35)

DIRECTIONS   Write "OK" after sentences with no **dangling clause.** Write "dangling OK" after sentences that have technically dangling clauses that are unobjectionable. Rephrase any sentence that has an awkward dangling clause.

EXAMPLES   When ripe, the oranges are picked and sorted.

OK

Speaking candidly, John is dishonest.

dangling OK

Reading the paper, a dog started barking.

While I was reading the paper, a dog started barking.

1. The dogs ran through the yard, chasing a rabbit.

2. The road is very crowded, going to work in the morning.

3. Being as familiar with the city as you are, it should be no problem to find that address.

4. Considering the number of people here, it's a wonder there is room for all.

5. Looking north from the top of the twin towers, Manhattan is spread out like a table-map.

6. Having returned safely from the jungle, all of our dangers now seemed like adventures.

7. Idly flipping through the book, my attention was caught by one of the illustrations.

8. Scattered by the wind, the yard was covered with dead leaves.

9. Turning back at the detour sign, we came home.

10. The congregation, carrying tambourines, danced down the aisle.

11.9 Semantic Diversity   (Ref: CGCE 11.21–36)

DIRECTIONS   Identify the semantic type of each italicized clause as one of the following: **time, place, condition, concession, cause, purpose, result, manner.** Write the appropriate term in the blank.

1. A 500-pound gorilla sleeps *wherever he wants.*   _____
2. *Although he likes to sail,* they are flying to Italy.   _____
3. *If you offer the monkey chocolate,* he'll do tricks.   _____
4. She couldn't open the trunk *because the key was lost.*   _____
5. She did the floor exercise *just as she had practiced it.*   _____
6. They spent a year in Germany *in order to learn German.*   _____
7. They spent a year in Germany, *so that they learned German.*   _____
8. *When you dance the hora,* you lock arms in a circle.   _____

DIRECTIONS   Rephrase each nonfinite or verbless clause to make specific some possible relationship between it and its superordinate clause.

EXAMPLE   John, soon to become a father, went to Mexico.

Because he was soon to become a father, *or* **Although . . . ,**

9. The girl, eager to be by herself, went to the skating rink.

_____

10. Washed and hung on the line to dry, the clothes were stolen by a tramp.

_____

11. Mullins erased the whole tape, trying to correct his mistake.

_____

12. Wilson, eventually to be president, was never a regular politician.

_____

13. Then at the height of her popularity, Isadora led a scandalous life.

_____

11.10   Comparative Sentences   (Ref: CGCE 11.37–44)

DIRECTIONS   Construct a **comparative sentence** based on each pair of questions and the comparative element indicated in parentheses.

EXAMPLE   How healthy is Jane? How healthy is her sister?   (more than)

Jane is healthier than her sister.

1. How soon will the movie start? How soon do you think it will start? (more than)

2. How many people wear hats these days? How many used to wear hats? (more than)

3. How many pets do they have? How many children do they have? (as as)

4. How many postmen drive trucks? How many postmen walk their rounds? (more than)

5. How often do I exercise? How often does anyone I know exercise? (less than)

6. How entertaining was the puzzle? How difficult was it?   (as as)

7. How dry were their clothes? Could they wear them?   (enough to)

8. How far away is the lion? Can we follow it?   (too to)

9. How far away is the lion? Can it follow us?   (too to)

10. How loud did they play the phonograph? Couldn't we talk?   (so that)

11. Are there tall pygmies? Is Niki [who is a pygmy] tall?   (more than)

12. Are there tall pygmies? Is Niki [who is not a pygmy] tall?   (more than)

11.11   Comment Clauses   (Ref: CGCE 11.45–46)

DIRECTIONS   Put parentheses around the **comment clause** in each sentence.

EXAMPLE   The Smiths, (as you know,) are going to England.

1. The clock is running slow, I suppose.
2. *Animal Farm,* as is generally recognized, is a political satire.
3. What is even more surprising, Columbus never realized that he had not reached Asia.
4. To give you a brief answer, no.
5. The extra vowel in "athaletic" is, using technical jargon, an example of anaptyxis.
6. Anaptyxis, put in simple terms, is the pronunciation of an extra vowel between consonants.

DIRECTIONS   Rephrase each sentence so that the main clause becomes a subordinate clause of comment:

EXAMPLE   I believe that at that time labor was cheap.

At that time, I believe, labor was cheap. _____

7. I hear that Guinevere has been seeing a good deal of Lancelot.

_____

8. I imagine that they will have a big bonfire.

_____

9. You know that it has been a long time since kings acted like that.

_____

10. It says in this book that Guinevere entered a nunnery.

_____

11. How do you suppose that Arthur found out?

_____

11.12   The Verb Phrase in Subordinate Clauses   (Ref: CGCE 11.47–51)

DIRECTIONS   Identify the time reference of the italicized verb as **past, present,** or **future.** Write the appropriate term in the blank.

1. He will go to Stockholm before they *award* the Nobel prizes.   _____

2. If it *rains* tomorrow, we will meet in the auditorium.   _____

3. You will have to leave the building when you *hear* the bell.   _____

4. You have to leave the building because I *hear* the bell.   _____

5. Let's suppose that the next manned rocket *goes* to Mars.   _____

6. If I *knew* the answer, I would tell you.   _____

7. If I *knew* the answer, I have forgotten it.   _____

8. I wish that I *had* a nice big hammock.   _____

9. I remember that I *had* a nice big hammock.   _____

10. The government is acting as though nothing *was* the matter.   _____

DIRECTIONS   Fill the blank with an appropriate form of the verb in parentheses.

11. English speakers (LIVE) _____ in America since the 1600s. 12. Since Oklahoma became a state, there (BE) _____ no Indian territory. 13. Before the Cherokees moved west, they (ORGANIZE) _____ as a nation. 14. After the Cherokees (SETTLE) _____ in Oklahoma, some of them returned to the eastern states. 15. Though he (BE) _____ a prophet, his neighbors will not listen to him. 16. If the truth (BE) _____ told, no one is completely guiltless. 17. It is important that every voter (BE) _____ well-informed. 18. He insisted that he (BE) _____ allowed to grow a mustache. 19. If the meeting (BE) _____ later, more people might get to it. 20. If the meeting (BE) _____ later, more people might have gotten to it. 21. He is talking as though he (HAVE) _____ his mouth full of marbles. 22. The tugboat will accompany the ocean liner as it (LEAVE) _____ the harbor. 23. The policeman (DIRECT) _____ traffic at this corner since early morning. 24. It is a shame that the play (CLOSE) _____ tomorrow.

168

11.13   Direct and Indirect Speech

(Ref: CGCE 11.52–58)

DIRECTIONS   Rewrite each sentence as **indirect speech.**

EXAMPLE   He said, "I am very angry."
He said that he was very angry.

1. She decided, "I am going to be in a parade."

   _____

2. Louise told George, "I hear you are moving now."

   _____

3. "I have lived here for a year," she added.

   _____

4. The newspaper reports: "There is a hurricane approaching Texas."

   _____

5. The interviewer asked me, "Why do you want to work for our company?"

   _____

6. The lecturer told us, "Absolute zero is −459.6° F."

   _____

7. "Are you comfortable?" the steward inquired.

   _____

8. "How late it has gotten!" the hostess thought.

   _____

9. He told us, "Bring bluebooks for the test."

   _____

10. She insisted, "He will have no trouble operating the machine."

    _____

11. The ticket seller warned us, "You can't find a seat."

    _____

12. The librarian told him, "We have no record of your book at this time."

    _____

11.14   Transferred Negation   (Ref: CGCE 11.58)

DIRECTIONS   Which of these sentences have paraphrases with the negative in the superordinate clauses, with no change of meaning? Write the paraphrases for those that do, and write "none" for those that have a different meaning when the negative is moved.

EXAMPLES   I suppose he hasn't paid yet.

I don't suppose he has paid yet.
_____

I say he hasn't paid yet.

none ("I don't say he has paid yet" differs in meaning)
_____

1. He hopes that the electricity won't go off.
_____

2. He believes that the electricity won't go off.
_____

3. He was afraid that the mail would not be on time.
_____

4. He supposed that the mail would not be on time.
_____

5. She expects that the robins have not gone south yet.
_____

6. She predicts that the robins have not gone south yet.
_____

7. They think that there is no ghost in the house.
_____

8. They maintain that there is no ghost in the house.
_____

9. I planned that there would be no difficulty.
_____

10. I figured that there would be no difficulty.
_____

● 12.1   Phrasal Verbs   (Ref: CGCE 12.2–3)

DIRECTIONS   Underline the **phrasal verbs.**

EXAMPLES   The children were <u>sitting down</u>.   We will <u>set</u> a new unit <u>up</u>.

1. The worst of the storm has blown over.
2. When the boy grows up, he plans to be a herpetologist.
3. Please stand by; we are having trouble with the audio.
4. You can drop in any time.
5. They don't get around as much as they used to.
6. The observers egged the boys on.
7. You will have to count me out.
8. When superstitious people drop a comb, they won't pick it up.
9. It is time to clean things up.
10. They hit it off when they first met.

DIRECTIONS   Replace the direct object noun phrase with a pronoun.

EXAMPLE   Drink up your milk quickly.

Drink it up quickly. _____

11. The ten-mile hike tired out the scouts.

_____

12. I have to write up a report tonight.

_____

13. She read over the speech ahead of time.

_____

14. The detective staked out the building.

_____

15. The heavyweight champion knocked out his opponent.

_____

12.2   Prepositional Verbs

(Ref: CGCE 12.4–5)

DIRECTIONS   Underline the **prepositional verbs.**

EXAMPLE   They <u>called on</u> the man.

1. We can do without sarcasm.
2. They got through the examination early.
3. The doctor swears by honey and vinegar.
4. She could pass for a native Swede.
5. He got over his cold.

DIRECTIONS   Indicate whether the italicized combination is a **phrasal verb** (PhV) or a **prepositional verb** (PrepV) by writing the appropriate abbreviation in the blank.

6. The applicant *filled out* the forms.   _____
7. The committee *talked about* their next meeting.   _____
8. The doctor *went into* pediatrics.   _____
9. The judge *put off* a decision.   _____
10. The lawyer is *running for* public office.   _____
11. The police *ran in* the tramp.   _____

DIRECTIONS   Indicate whether each sentence contains a **prepositional verb** (PrepV) or a **verb** plus a **prepositional phrase** (V + PP).

12. He ran into the street.   _____
13. He ran into an old friend.   _____
14. She will stand by her former statement.   _____
15. She will stand by the front door.   _____
16. They went through a lot of trouble.   _____
17. They went through a lot of countries.   _____

12.3   Phrasal-Prepositional and Other Verbs   (Ref: CGCE 12.2–6)

DIRECTIONS   Indicate whether each sentence contains a **phrasal verb** (PhV), a **prepositional verb** (PrepV), a **verb** plus **prepositional phrase** (V + PP), or a **phrasal-prepositional verb** (Ph-PrepV) by writing the appropriate abbreviation in the blank.

EXAMPLES   They turned on the television.   **PhV**

The mad dog turned on his master.   **PrepV**

The car turned on the street.   **V + PP**

They have turned on to classical jazz.   **Ph-PrepV**

1. She put up with the minor inconvenience.   _____

2. She put up preserved cherries.   _____

3. It finally comes to a matter of taste.   _____

4. He finally came to.   _____

5. They are finally coming to Chicago.   _____

6. She ran down the hill.   _____

7. She ran down her neighbor.   _____

8. The clock ran down.   _____

9. He got around the problem.   _____

10. He got around to the book.   _____

11. They went through the corridor.   _____

12. They went through the newspaper.   _____

13. They went through with their plans.   _____

14. He turned in his bed.   _____

15. He turned in his report.   _____

16. He tuned in to his favorite program.   _____

17. They looked into every nook and cranny.   _____

18. They looked into the problem.   _____

19. She goes in for water sports.   _____

20. She goes for mystery novels.   _____

12.4 Verbs and Transitivity (Ref: CGCE 12.7–10)

DIRECTIONS   Underline the verb in each sentence and indicate whether it is an **intransitive** (I), **transitive** (T), **current copula** (C), or **resulting copula** (R) by writing the appropriate letter in the blank.

EXAMPLES   The tomatoes <u>are growing</u> well.   **I**

He <u>is growing</u> tomatoes.   **T**

John <u>was</u> a doctor.   **C**

John <u>became</u> a doctor.   **R**

1. Trollope's novels read easily. _____

2. Nell read all of Trollope's novels last year. _____

3. Nell reads aloud in a good clear voice. _____

4. She endorsed the check with purple ink. _____

5. She sneezed because of the pepper. _____

6. The kite flew well in the breeze. _____

7. Burt flew the kite without a tail. _____

8. The actress slowly turned toward the audience. _____

9. Orson turned the doorknob very slowly. _____

10. Mortimer seems an unlikely candidate for mayor. _____

11. Louella remains the only woman astronaut in the program. _____

12. The bear stayed quiet all winter. _____

13. The plane from Iceland is on time. _____

14. Black certainly becomes Sadie. _____

15. Julia became a first-rate French chef. _____

16. The witness turned pale during the cross-examination. _____

17. Suddenly the guardsman went limp. _____

18. We went to Buckingham Palace for an outing. _____

19. The burglar alarm sounded. _____

20. The piano sounds out of tune. _____

21. The watchman sounded the alarm. _____

12.5 Adjective Complementation   (Ref: CGCE 12.11–13)

DIRECTIONS Complete each sentence by making a **complement** for the adjective out of the expression in parentheses.

EXAMPLE They are conscious . . . (their responsibility)
They are conscious of their responsibility.

1. They became aware . . .   (a knocking on the door)

_____

2. He was intent . . .   (watch the car races)

_____

3. She is familiar . . .   (the rules of chess)

_____

4. Harry was amazed . . .   (his own success)

_____

5. We were positive . . .   (the car runs)

_____

6. The judge was insistent . . .   (the jury is informed)

_____

7. The usher was good . . .   (he helped the lost child)

_____

8. Rich was quick . . .   (he notices things quickly)

_____

9. Zoe was pleased . . .   (it pleased her to be Miss America)

_____

10. Albert feels reluctant . . .   (he doesn't want to eat squid)

_____

11. The puzzle is easy . . .   (to solve the puzzle is easy)

_____

12. A fur coat is hot . . .   (to wear a fur coat in summer makes one hot)

_____

12.6   Direct Objects

(Ref: CGCE 12.14–27)

DIRECTIONS   Put parentheses around the **direct objects.** If the direct object is a clause, it may have its own direct object.

EXAMPLE   Tom decided **(**that they should meet **(**her.**))**

1. Please don't use the air conditioner during peak afternoon hours.
2. The leading man directed himself in the play.
3. She wore an old pair of faded dungarees.
4. They have decided when to hold the match.
5. The handicappers agree that the horse has no chance.
6. They plan to see a double feature.
7. He finally stopped hiccupping.
8. We expect you to like this book.
9. I heard the shutter bang once.
10. They admire his defending the underdog.
11. Taxi drivers want partitions installed between the seats.
12. She tie-dyed the shirt purple and yellow.
13. They crowned him King of the Swedes.

DIRECTIONS   Indicate whether the italicized expression is a **direct object** (O) or a **subject complement** (C) by writing the appropriate abbreviation in the blank.

14. He grew *more tomatoes* in his garden this year.   _____
15. He grew *more curious* as the day went on.   _____
16. She made *a really excellent nurse.*   _____
17. She made *a really excellent soufflé.*   _____
18. He felt (like) *a stranger* even in his own home.   _____
19. He felt *a stranger* (was) somewhere in the room.   _____
20. He weighed *150 pounds.*   _____
21. He weighed *150 packages.*   _____

12.7   Clauses as Direct Objects (1)   (Ref: CGCE 12.17–27)

DIRECTIONS   Complete each sentence by making the material in parentheses into a **finite clause direct object**.

1. They realized . . .   (a piece of the puzzle was lost)

_____

2. She found out . . .   (what did he want?)

_____

3. He rejoiced . . .   .   (the term was over)

_____

4. I suggest . . .   (he takes a trip)

_____

5. We wonder . . .   (have the astronauts landed?)

_____

DIRECTIONS   Complete each sentence by making the material in parentheses into a **nonfinite clause**, functioning as **direct object**.

6. He needs . . .   (he should watch)

_____

7. He needs . . .   (someone should watch him)

_____

8. She remembered . . .   (she was to return the book and did so)

_____

9. She remembered . . .   (she had returned the book)

_____

10. They are learning . . .   (they roller-skate)

_____

11. We will soon finish . . .   (we are memorizing dates)

_____

12.8   Clauses as Direct Objects (2)   (Ref: CGCE 12.18–27)

DIRECTIONS   Complete each sentence by making the material in parentheses into a **nonfinite clause,** functioning as **direct object.**

1. I like . . .   (I live in the mountains)

_____

2. Dave supposed . . .   (his brother was at home)

_____

3. Murray expected . . .   (the theater would give free passes)

_____

4. Polly waited for . . .   (the telephone rang three times)

_____

5. High places make . . .   (that mountain climber feels dizzy)

_____

6. No one saw . . .   (the pot boiled over)

_____

7. We risked . . .   (they might find out)

_____

8. He liked . . .   (the band would end with a Sousa march)

_____

9. They caught . . .   (Zoe violated curfew again)

_____

10. The doorman heard . . .   (someone asked for a cab)

_____

11. The photographer wanted . . .   (his film should be developed)

_____

12. They saw . . .   (the city was bombed)

_____

13. The drill left . . .   (the team was exhausted)

_____

12.9   Verbless Clauses as Complements   (Ref: CGCE 12.26–27)

DIRECTIONS   Complete each sentence by making the material in parentheses into a **verbless clause** (that is, a **direct object** and **object complement**).

EXAMPLE   I consider . . .   (John is a good driver)
   I consider John a good driver.

1. The sergeant called . . .   (Gomer was the best soldier in the squad)

2. We always keep . . .   (the coffee is ready)

3. The umpire declared . . .   (the runner was safe)

4. The acting school made . . .   (Marlon became a method actor)

5. The architect intended . . .   (the building was for public use)

6. No one recognized . . . as . . .   (the stranger was a celebrity)

7. They mistook . . . for . . .   (the maître d' is not a waiter)

DIRECTIONS   Write the intensive clause that corresponds to the direct object plus object complement combination in each sentence.

EXAMPLE   He made Martha his secretary.
   Martha is his secretary.

8. The news has left us confused.

9. We want a tape recorder handy.

10. They consider the book a classic.

12.10   Passives and Transitivity (1)   (Ref: CGCE 12.15–27)

DIRECTIONS   Write the corresponding **passive** for each sentence that has one. If there is no passive, write "none."

1. They have captured only one tiger with the net.

   _____

2. They have captured only one tiger with white fur.

   _____

3. They sailed a raft made of papyrus across the Atlantic.

   _____

4. That reminds me of a story.

   _____

5. Thunder and lightning mean rain.

   _____

6. This book lacks an index.

   _____

7. The fur coat doesn't fit her.

   _____

8. They categorically denied that the election had been rigged.

   _____

9. Someone has questioned whether the national anthem should be changed.

   _____

10. Jerry decided to become an orthodontist.

   _____

11. They chose Victoria to sing the lead in *Aïda*.

   _____

12. Someone observed the suspect enter the bank.

   _____

13. I prefer my steak to be well-done.

   _____

12.11   Passives and Transitivity (2)   (Ref: CGCE 12.15–29)

DIRECTIONS   Write the corresponding **passive** for each sentence. If more than one passive is possible for any sentence, write both.

1. Everyone enjoyed Hank's breaking the record.

   _____

2. They kept the bottle filled with ice water.

   _____

3. They voted Chiquita "Miss Miami."

   _____

4. Everyone found the problem very difficult.

   _____

5. That can save you a lot of work.

   _____

6. Everyone congratulated him on his election.

   _____

7. People always make fun of politicians.

   _____

   _____

8. You should pay attention to the directions.

   _____

9. They assured the judge that the jury was hung.

   _____

10. They encouraged Rhoda to take the exam.

    _____

11. The pitcher threw the catcher a practice ball.

    _____

    _____

12. They sent Albert a registered letter.

    _____

    _____

13. They allowed Molly an extra turn.

    _____

    _____

12.12   Indirect Objects   (Ref: CGCE 12.28–32)

DIRECTIONS   Underline **direct objects** once and **indirect objects** twice.

1. She got the poor dog a bone.
2. Do yourself a favor.
3. Ask me no questions.
4. I'll tell you no lies.
5. Going over Niagara Falls in a barrel taught him a lesson.
6. Her friends gave the bride a party.
7. Her friends gave the bride a present.
8. The salesman showed his customer the newest model.
9. They offer students a discount.
10. The reporter sent his editor a story.

DIRECTIONS   Rewrite the above sentences, replacing the indirect objects with prepositional phrases.

1. _____

2. _____

3. _____

4. _____

5. _____

6. _____

7. _____

8. _____

9. _____

10. _____

● 13.1   Complex Noun Phrases (1)   (Ref: CGCE 13.1)

DIRECTIONS   Combine the sentences in each set into a single sentence with a **complex noun phrase** as subject.

EXAMPLE   The girl is Mary Smith.   The girl is standing in the corner.
          The girl is pretty.   The girl is standing alone.

The pretty girl standing alone in the corner is Mary Smith.

1. The house was being painted.   The house was wooden.
   The house was old.   The house was nearby.

2. The man signed his name.   The man was dressed casually.
   The man was wearing glasses.   The glasses had steel rims.

3. A landslide buried the hut.   The landslide was on Bald Mountain.
   A hunter started the landslide.   The landslide was destructive.

4. The sweater had a tear in it.   She was wearing the sweater.
   The sweater was cashmere.   The sweater was her sister's.
   The sweater was blue.   The sweater was from Bergdorf's.

5. The telephone was ringing.   The telephone was in the lobby.
   The telephone was free.   I was waiting in the lobby.
   The telephone was public.   The telephone was new.

6. The puzzle had a piece missing.   The puzzle was Chinese.
   The puzzle was difficult.   He was working the puzzle.
   The puzzle was of rings.   He was without success.

13.2   Complex Noun Phrases (2)   (Ref: CGCE 13.1–2)

DIRECTIONS   Circle the **head** in each **complex noun phrase**, then write the simple sentences that are implied by the complex phrase.

EXAMPLE   the young ⊙girl in the corner who became angry

The girl was young.

The girl was in the corner.

The girl became angry.

1. an old silent movie from the twenties starring Rudolph Valentino

   _____

   _____

   _____

2. the bright new copper penny that he found

   _____

   _____

   _____

3. the highly recommended Chinese doctor from Chicago whom he consulted, an acupuncturist

   _____

   _____

   _____

   _____

4. a soft white knitted shawl, fringed with blue

   _____

   _____

   _____

13.3 Restrictiveness and Permanency (Ref: CGCE 13.3–4)

DIRECTIONS Indicate whether the italicized modifier is **restrictive** (R) or **nonrestrictive** (N) by writing the appropriate letter in the blank. Then punctuate the nonrestrictive modifiers with commas.

1. Milton *who is their best friend* will help them. _____

2. Anyone *who can't bluff* shouldn't play poker. _____

3. They saw the Luigi *who runs a pizza parlor on Main.* _____

4. They saw Luigi *who never eats at his own restaurant.* _____

5. The twin *who was born first* looks more like her mother. _____

6. The elder twin *who looks more like her mother* is Mary. _____

7. The finger *on which she wears the ring* is the little finger of her right hand. _____

8. She broke the little finger of her right hand *on which she wears the ring.* _____

9. Our waiter *who was wearing a red coat* has disappeared. _____

10. The food *that we ordered* must be ready now. _____

DIRECTIONS Indicate whether the italicized modifier is **temporary** (T) or **permanent** (P) by writing the appropriate letter in the blank.

11. The librarian is *alone.* _____

12. The *solitary* librarian is busy. _____

13. The neighbors are *nearby.* _____

14. The *nearby* neighbors are away. _____

15. The *next* house is brick. _____

16. The brick house is *next.* _____

17. The stars are *agleam* like candles tonight. _____

18. The *gleaming* stars are fading in the dawn. _____

19. The assignment is *complete* now. _____

20. The *complete* assignment will take a while. _____

13.4   Restrictive Relative Clauses   (Ref: CGCE 13.5–10)

DIRECTIONS   Combine the two sentences by inserting the second into the first as a **restrictive relative clause.** Use the relative *that* whenever possible, but put *that* in parentheses if the relative might be omitted. Be prepared to discuss what other relatives might be used in the sentences.

EXAMPLE   The boy is Richard. We met him.

The boy (that) we met is Richard.

1. The newsboy is collecting. He brings the morning paper.

2. The tires are steel-belted. We just bought them.

3. The job was at a hardware store. The job appealed to her.

4. Someone handed me a rose. I never saw him before.

5. The table had been recently painted. He put the book on it.

6. The person knew all the details. We heard the story from him.

7. Monday is the day. He plays golf on that day.

8. The reason is simple. Ice floats for a reason.

9. Rain was the cause. The game was called for a cause.

10. You are welcome to share such food. We have such food.

13.5 Nonrestrictive Relative Clauses   (Ref: CGCE 13.5–7, 11–12)

DIRECTIONS   Combine the two sentences by inserting the second into the first as a **nonrestrictive relative clause.** Use one of the relatives *who, whom, whose, which, where, when, why.*

EXAMPLE   Then he met Mary. She invited him to a party.

Then he met Mary, who invited him to a party.

1. The radio needs batteries. It is a portable.

2. Hume was a Scotsman. He brought empiricism to its logical conclusion.

3. Men and monkeys are distinguished by the power of speech. They are biologically kin.

4. The Sphinx asked Oedipus a riddle. The Sphinx has a lion's body and a woman's head.

5. Secretariat won the triple crown. Secretariat is one of racing's fastest horses.

6. The movie was filmed in black and white. Its director was a Swede.

7. Pandora was very curious. The box was given to her.

8. New York is the largest American city. The UN is located in New York.

9. The Renaissance was a time of great literary activity. Shakespeare wrote during the Renaissance.

10. He stands on his head while he studies. That amuses her.

13.6   Relative and Appositive Clauses   (Ref: CGCE 13.5–13)

DIRECTIONS   Combine the two sentences by inserting the second into the first as a **relative** (R) or **appositive** (A) clause. Indicate which kind of clause the second sentence becomes by writing the appropriate letter in the blank.

EXAMPLE   The belief is well founded. It is that no one is infallible.   **A**

The belief that no one is infallible is well founded.

1. The answer surprised us. He gave the answer.   _____

2. The answer surprised us. The answer was that he didn't know.   _____

3. The pilot made an announcement. It was that we were landing.   _____

4. The pilot made an announcement. It calmed the passengers.   _____

5. He sent in a request. It was that they play "Melancholy Baby."   _____

6. He sent in a request. It could not be filled.   _____

7. The best suggestion was made by Tim. It was that the committee disband.   _____

8. The best suggestion was made by Tim. It also pleased us.   _____

9. He has orders. They are that he is to leave.   _____

10. He has orders. He is to leave the orders.   _____

13.7 Postmodification by Nonfinite Clauses (Ref: CGCE 13.14–18)

DIRECTIONS Rephrase each sentence so that it has a **nonfinite clause** as postmodifier.

EXAMPLE The man who was writing the obituary is my friend.
The man writing the obituary is my friend.

1. The man who reports the weather is a meteorologist.

_____

2. Quigly Throckmorton, who wore jodhpurs, was the center of attention.

_____

3. The train that will be arriving tonight will be the last this month.

_____

4. The piano that is being tuned is an upright.

_____

5. Books that are sold on the newsstand are not available in the library.

_____

6. The front door, which is hidden by shrubbery, is hard to see.

_____

7. The book that you need to read is this new spy story.

_____

8. The subject that Lisa should study is ikebana.

_____

9. The way in which one ought to eat sukiyaki is with chopsticks.

_____

10. Laputa, which is to be admitted to the UN next month, is unstable.

_____

11. The suggestion that we should play pool was made by Harold.

_____

12. The best motion, that the meeting should adjourn, came last.

_____

13.8 Postmodification by Prepositional Phrases (Ref: CGCE 13.19–23)

DIRECTIONS   Reword each noun phrase so that the **prepositional phrase** is replaced by a **relative clause.**

1. the picture on the wall

2. the TV program after the news

3. a novel like *Tom Jones*

4. the artist as a young man

5. a cat with white paws

6. a man of few pretensions

7. the only commercial, for a soap powder

8. the *Mass in B Minor,* by Bach

DIRECTIONS   Reword each noun phrase as a sentence.

9. John's fear of high places

10. the comedian's imitation of the mayor

11. her reading of the play

12. their disagreement about the play

13.9   Minor Types of Postmodification   (Ref: CGCE 13.24)

DIRECTIONS   Underline the noun-phrase postmodifier and indicate whether it is an **adverbial modifier** (Av), a **postposed adjective** (Aj), or a **"mode" qualifier** (M) by writing the appropriate letter in the blank.

1. She is leaving on Monday, and he is arriving the day after.   _____

2. She met someone new last night.   _____

3. The inspector general is visiting soon.   _____

4. The watchdog, little but fierce, attacked the burglar.   _____

5. The house next door is for rent.   _____

6. They served peas and potatoes lyonnaise.   _____

7. Twenty-two of the tarot cards are the trumps major.   _____

8. The trip there was a pleasant one.   _____

9. Her dress, stylishly short, was pleated.   _____

10. It is an epic à la Hollywood.   _____

DIRECTIONS   Rewrite each sentence to reduce the relative clause to a minor type of postmodification.

11. She left her book on the chair that is right here.

_____

12. He asked the librarian for something that is entertaining.

_____

13. They have proof that is positive of his innocence.

_____

14. There are nations that are smaller than Rhode Island.

_____

15. We are having shrimp that are cooked in the creole manner for supper.

_____

13.10 Multiple Postmodification (Ref: CGCE 13.25–26)

DIRECTIONS Combine the expressions into a single noun phrase with multiple **postmodification.**

EXAMPLE the woman in the corner the woman talking to John
the woman in the corner talking to John

1. the book that he needs to read the book from the library

2. the bus waiting at the stop the bus to town the stop across the street

3. the lecture on hydrodynamics the lecture last week the reading assignment on hydrodynamics the reading assignment last week

4. the stained-glass window with the crack the stained-glass window in the middle

5. the stained glass window with the crack the crack in the middle of the window

6. the rain that the weatherman predicted the rain that we were to have

7. the quickest way to go to Paris the quickest way that we have discovered the quickest way other than flying

8. the book that we are supposed to read the instructor said that we are supposed to read the book

9. the man who will be delivering the mail they think that man will be delivering the mail

13.11   Premodification

(Ref: CGCE 13.27–35)

DIRECTIONS   Omitting determiners, put parentheses around each premodifying item (single word or word group) and indicate whether it is an **adjective** (Aj), **participle** (P), **genitive** (G), **noun** (N), **adverbial** (Av), or **clause** (C) by writing the appropriate abbreviation in the blank.

EXAMPLES   I visited his (delightful) cottage.   **Aj**

I visited his (crumbling) cottage.   **P**

I visited his (fisherman's) cottage.   **G**

I visited his (country) cottage.   **N**

I visited his (far-away) cottage.   **Av**

I visited his (pop-down-for-the-weekend) cottage.   **C**

1. San Francisco is a long way to go for supper.   _____

2. He was known as the singing cabbie.   _____

3. She wanted to go to a girls' school.   _____

4. Just follow the gravel path through the park.   _____

5. You mustn't go down the up staircase.   _____

6. He gave us one of those "I've got your number" looks.   _____

7. The sound of the ringing bell woke him.   _____

8. History is more than the study of long-ago wars.   _____

9. Philippa joined a consumers' cooperative recently.   _____

10. That station plays get-up-and-go music.   _____

11. We have to wait for the dismissal bell to leave.   _____

12. I had a funny dream yesterday.   _____

13. She was wearing a blue peasant's skirt.   _____ _____

14. He is a once winner of the bridge tournament.   _____ _____

15. He has another involved do-it-yourself project.   _____ _____

16. He gave a long, lingering look at the pie.   _____ _____

17. Have you tried bird's nest soup?   _____ _____

13.12   Premodifiers and Postmodifiers   (Ref: CGCE 13.27–35)

DIRECTIONS   Revise each noun phrase to make the **postmodifier** wholly or partly into a **premodifier**.

EXAMPLE   that story which was really quite unbelievable
that really quite unbelievable story

1. a horse that was so fast

_____

2. directions that are easy to follow

_____

3. an argument that convinces

_____

4. a politician who shakes hands

_____

5. the floor that was swept recently

_____

6. London Bridge, which has been reconstructed

_____

7. a collar that is the sort worn by ministers

_____

8. the meeting that is for new students

_____

9. the chairman who then was

_____

10. a movie that is in its first run

_____

11. a chance that comes once in a lifetime

_____

13.13   Multiple Premodification   (Ref: CGCE 13.36–39)

DIRECTIONS   Omitting determiners, bracket the elements in each noun phrase to show the structure of the phrase. (Brackets of different shapes can be used as a visual aid—the shape has no significance, but both brackets in a pair must be of the same shape.)

EXAMPLES   his [last (brilliant book)]

the [new (table and chairs)]

his < { really [quite (unbelievably delightful)] } cottage >

1.   the   first   ten   prizes

2.   the   ten   first   prizes

3.   a   fast   working   detergent

4.   a   fast   touring   car

5.   a   determined,   dedicated   public   servant

6.   his   close   friends   and   acquaintances

7.   the   next   morning   and   afternoon

8.   a   quite   amazingly   short   time

9.   those   so   very   convincing   explanations

10.   these   children's   education

11.   these   child's   spoons

12.   a   very   tall   German   woman's   furniture

13.   city   hall   officials

14.   automatic   corn   popper

15.   metropolitan   Atlanta   rapid   transit   authority

16.   a   plastic   paper   back   book   cover

17.   strategic   arms   limitation   talks

18.   late   fall   and   winter   rains

19.   dark   eyed   women

20.   red   or   blond   bearded   men

13.14   Order of Modifiers

(Ref: CGCE 13.40–43)

DIRECTIONS   Make a noun phrase from each group of words, arranging the pre-modifiers in their most natural sequence.

1. French political scene the uncertain

_____

2. chemistry Chinese eager our students young

_____

3. antique Italian marble statues those white

_____

4. a brown iron old pipe rusting useless

_____

5. spring running clear fresh lovely water

_____

DIRECTIONS   Rephrase to make related modifiers continuous. Be prepared to discuss which sentences are better with continuous modifiers and which are better with dis-continuous ones.

6. I read a book yesterday that amazed me.

_____

7. Superficially it was a convincing explanation.

_____

8. A book was written describing her childhood last year.

_____

9. He ordered a hot cup of coffee and a gooey kind of dessert.

_____

10. I heard a longer story than she told from the last person to arrive.

_____

11. The new supervisor in our department is a hard person to please.

_____

● **14.1 Information Focus** (Ref: CGCE 14.2–7, App II.7)

DIRECTIONS Underline the word, or part of the word, that is most probably the **information focus** in each **information unit**. The end of each information unit is marked with a vertical bar.

EXAMPLE Dylan Thomas was born in <u>Swansea</u>.|

1. McDonald spent his vacation in the Catskills.|
2. McDonald went to the Catskills for his vacation.|
3. Their dog bit the mailman.|
4. Their dog bit the mailman in the leg.|
5. Their dog bit the mailman in the leg yesterday.|
6. The mailman was bitten by their dog.|
7. Do you want a pepperoni pizza,| or an anchovy?|
8. There are laws governing immigration,| not emigration.|
9. Portland, Oregon, is where he moved,| rather than Portland, Maine.|
10. She left the book on the desk,| or somewhere near it.|

DIRECTIONS Underline the word or word part that is the information focus in each response, and put parentheses around the part of the response that is **new information**.

EXAMPLE [What are we doing?] We're (going to the <u>races</u>.)

11. [What did Simon hide under the rug?] Simon hid his money under the rug.
12. [Who hid his money under the rug?] Simon hid his money under the rug.
13. [Where did Simon hide his money?] Simon hid his money under the rug.
14. [What did Simon do?] Simon hid his money under the rug.
15. [What happened?] Simon hid his money under the rug.
16. [Emma didn't spill the soup.] Emma did spill the soup.
17. [Turn on the light.] I've already turned it on.
18. [The keys aren't in the car.] The keys must be in the car.

14.2   **End-Focus and End-Weight**   (Ref: CGCE 14.8–9)

DIRECTIONS   Rephrase these sentences to accord with the principles of **end-focus** and **end-weight** by reversing their **voice:**

EXAMPLE   Ercol makes them.

      They're made by Ercol.

1. A bald actor with a white beard played the role.

2. The General Manufacturing Corporation hired her.

3. The escaped convict was recaptured by the police.

4. The stock-car races in Bakersville were reported by him.

5. That anyone would watch three TV games in a row amused her.

6. That there might be a leak in the gas line worried them.

DIRECTIONS   Rephrase each sentence as its **converse.**

EXAMPLE   An uncle benefitted from the will.

      The will benefitted an uncle.

7. A man dressed in a caftan and a burnoose sold it to me.

8. A large picture magazine was on top of the book.

9. A long speech about ecology preceded the entertainment.

10. A man carrying a box of eggs tripped over the cat.

14.3   Theme and Inversion   (Ref: CGCE 14.10–14)

DIRECTIONS   Put parentheses around the **theme** in each clause.

EXAMPLES   (He) bought a new house.|
            (Which house) did he buy?|

1. The bulletin board is covered with announcements.|
2. They ought to have someone clear it off.|
3. Where are you going over the holidays?|
4. Whose dirty socks are these under my bed?|
5. Can you swim underwater?|
6. Tell me what the assignment for tomorrow is.|
7. The first one to leave, was he?|
8. Treasurer they elected him?|
9. Into the house you go!|
10. The book she found entertaining;| the movie she grew tired of.|
11. Away went the hounds, after the rabbit.|
12. Before us lay a great canyon.|
13. "In no case should you open the box,"| warned Prometheus.|
14. May heaven help you,| should you ignore this warning.|
15. Kindhearted as she is,| she can't hurt a mouse.|
16. Scarcely is heard a discouraging word.|
17. Barely had the game begun| when they made a touchdown.|
18. Receiving the ball is Stanley Kotowski.|
19. Try as they might,| they couldn't make the down.|
20. Never before have I heard such balderdash.|

14.4   Cleft Sentences

DIRECTIONS   For each sentence, write the corresponding **cleft sentence**, focusing the italicized item.

EXAMPLE   John wore his best suit *last night*.

It was last night that John wore his best suit.
_____

1. *Augusta* played the flute with the school band last year.
_____

2. Augusta played *the flute* with the school band last year.
_____

3. Augusta played the flute *with the school band* last year.
_____

4. Augusta played the flute with *the school band* last year.
_____

5. Augusta played the flute with the school band *last year*.
_____

6. Jude sent his laundry to *his sister in Boise*.
_____

7. We were on the beach at Acapulco *just yesterday*.
_____

8. They spent the winter in *Saint Tropez* last year.
_____

9. Did Simon study Russian *in order to be a diplomat?*
_____

10. We are not digging this ditch *for him*.
_____

11. *The music to an old Scottish song* was used for the anthem.
_____

14.5   Pseudo-Cleft Sentences   (Ref: CGCE 14.17)

DIRECTIONS   For each sentence write the corresponding **pseudo-cleft sentences,** focusing the italicized item. Write two pseudo-cleft paraphrases for each sentence.

EXAMPLE   You need *a good rest.*

A good rest is what you need.

What you need is a good rest.

1. George chopped down *the apple tree.*

2. *George* chopped down the apple tree.

3. George *chopped down the apple tree.*

4. They *were playing tic-tac-toe.*

5. He *has lost the car key.*

6. She found a silver dollar *last week.*

7. He found his pen *right where he left it.*

14.6 Another Kind of Thematic Paraphrase (Ref: CGCE 14.18)

DIRECTIONS Following the pattern in the example, write paraphrases for each sentence.

EXAMPLE To teach her is a pleasure.

It is a pleasure to teach her.

She is a pleasure to teach.

1. To watch Arnold playing golf is an education.

   _____

   _____

2. To compete with him is not easy.

   _____

   _____

3. To explain laser beams is a problem.

   _____

   _____

4. To use spitballs is illegal.

   _____

   _____

5. That nations will disagree is certain.

   _____

   _____

6. That all the continents were originally one is likely.

   _____

   _____

7. That Mona is winning the race appears to be the case.

   _____

   _____

14.7   Existential Sentences

(Ref: CGCE 14.19–22)

DIRECTIONS   Rephrase each sentence as an **existential sentence.**

EXAMPLES   Something must be wrong.
There must be something wrong.

Something keeps upsetting him.
There is something that keeps upsetting him.

1. Someone to see you is outside.

   _____

2. Nothing is funnier than a kitten with a string.

   _____

3. A lot of horses are racing.

   _____

4. Fires and floods have always been [existed].

   _____

5. A building was torn down on Main Street.

   _____

6. Is something bothering you?

   _____

7. Some stores are staying open all night, aren't they?

   _____

8. A tree fell across the road.

   _____

9. Benjy wants us to do something for him.

   _____

10. A day will come when solar energy is the main power source.

    _____

11. A cab never happens to be around when you want one.

    _____

NAME_____   SCORE _____

14.8 Existential Sentences with HAVE   (Ref: CGCE 14.23)

DIRECTIONS Rephrase each sentence, first as an existential sentence with *there* +
BE, and then as an existential sentence with HAVE.

EXAMPLE   Several friends of his are in China.
There are several friends of his in China.
He has several friends in China.

1. A few of her classes were canceled.

2. A shoestring is in my soup.

3. Some fleas are bothering that dog.

4. A good many reasons for his disliking TV exist.

DIRECTIONS Rephrase each sentence as an existential sentence with HAVE.

5. Samson's hair was cut off.

6. Walter's classes are all in this building.

7. My car ran out of gas on me.

14.9 Extraposition

DIRECTIONS   For each sentence, write a paraphrase with **extraposition.**

EXAMPLE   That she put arsenic in his tea is possible.

It is possible that she put arsenic in his tea.

1. Whether or not she has a driver's license makes a difference.

2. For you to say that is easy.

3. That a UFO landed in Times Square has been rumored.

4. Just to watch the weight-lifters made him tired.

5. To read about herself in the paper gave her a thrill.

6. Where you live doesn't matter.

7. Seeing her after so long was good.

8. They believe to enforce the laws is necessary.

9. Someone leaked that there had been a secret meeting to the newspapers.

10. Do you think being a professional student is easy?

11. For George to be there on time is important. [i.e., important to us]

12. To be there on time is important for George. [i.e., for us to be there]

14.10 Other Kinds of Postponement (Ref: CGCE 14.28–32)

DIRECTIONS   Reword each sentence, **postponing** some item to achieve end-focus or end-weight.

EXAMPLE   They pronounced every one of the accused except the man who had sounded the alarm guilty.

They pronounced guilty every one of the accused except the man who had sounded the alarm.

1. They elected the person who seemed best qualified to hold the office president.

   _____

2. He asked whoever he thought might have been there about the accident.

   _____

3. She sent the first school to offer her a scholarship an acceptance.

   _____

4. The theater had to turn almost a hundred persons away.

   _____

5. A report that the Premier had resigned was circulating.

   _____

6. What opportunity to rob the safe did the defendant have?

   _____

7. Marsha herself baked the bread.

   _____

8. The critics wrote more than they ever had before about his last novel.

   _____

9. COMSAT makes better communications than we used to have with Asia possible.

   _____

10. Everybody except Felix was there.

   _____

14.11 Structural Compensation; Emotive Emphasis
(Ref: CGCE 14.33–38)

DIRECTIONS Paraphrase each sentence to **stretch** the predicate.

EXAMPLE He sang.

He was singing. *or* **He sang some songs.** _____

1. He read. _____

2. She walked. _____

3. He swims. _____

4. She babysits. _____

DIRECTIONS Paraphrase each sentence to give emotive emphasis or reinforcement.

EXAMPLES You look a wreck.

You do look a wreck. _____

These politicians are all the same.

They're all the same, these politicians. _____

5. He surprised us.

_____

6. They had a good time.

_____

7. Don't dither.

_____

8. It's much too soon.

_____

9. That man who came to see you this morning about insurance is back.

_____

10. Those Joneses are hard to keep up with.

_____

App I.1   Prefixation

(Ref: CGCE App I.2–12; WNCD)

DIRECTIONS   A **prefix** seldom changes the part of speech of a word, but only modifies its meaning. Separate the prefix from the rest of the word with a slash. Be prepared to identify the meaning of each prefix.

EXAMPLES   arch/duke   fore/tell   un/fair

1. amoral
2. antebellum
3. antitrust
4. autohypnosis
5. bifocal
6. circumnavigate
7. cisatlantic
8. copilot
9. counterclaim
10. cryptocommunist
11. deplane
12. demigod
13. disarm
14. exwife
15. extramarital
16. hyperactive

17. insecure
18. intertwine
19. intravenous
20. malnutrition
21. microwave
22. midweek
23. minitheater
24. misspeak
25. monosyllable
26. multihued
27. neoisolationism
28. nonstop
29. panhellenic
30. paramedical
31. polyandrous
32. postgraduate

33. prepay
34. preternatural
35. pro-British
36. protoplasm
37. pseudoprophet
38. reproduce
39. retroactive
40. semimonthly
41. stepbrother
42. subtitle
43. supermarket
44. surcharge
45. transplant
46. triangle
47. ultraviolet
48. uniform

DIRECTIONS   A few prefixes are characteristic of a part of speech. Separate the prefix from the rest of the word with a slash, identify the part of speech of each word, and give another word with the same prefix.

49. askew   _____

50. befriend   _____

51. enlarge   _____

App I.2   Suffixation

(Ref: CGCE App I.13–22)

DIRECTIONS   Most **suffixes** are characteristic of parts of speech. Separate the suffix from the rest of the word with a slash, and indicate the part of speech it characterizes.

EXAMPLES   gang/ster _____**noun**_____   virtu/ous _____**adjective**_____

1. changeable _____
2. postage _____
3. recital _____
4. global _____
5. Tibetan _____
6. dietary _____
7. pastorate _____
8. proportionate _____
9. hyphenate _____
10. taxation _____
11. appointee _____
12. profiteer _____
13. woolen _____
14. dampen _____
15. persistence _____
16. tendency _____
17. teacher _____
18. Japanese _____
19. heiress _____
20. novelette _____
21. hopeful _____
22. spoonful _____
23. girlhood _____

24. poetic _____
25. purify _____
26. stylish _____
27. symbolism _____
28. purist _____
29. humanity _____
30. secretive _____
31. legalize _____
32. hairless _____
33. ladylike _____
34. beastly _____
35. nicely _____
36. statement _____
37. firmness _____
38. rivalry _____
39. kinship _____
40. awesome _____
41. growth _____
42. pressure _____
43. backwards _____
44. clockwise _____
45. soapy _____
46. honesty _____

App I.3 Conversion

(Ref: CGCE App I.23–31)

DIRECTIONS   **Conversion** is the use of a word as a part of speech other than that which it primarily is. For each word, write two sentences, using the word as different parts of speech in each.

1. care _____

   _____

2. clear _____

   _____

3. up _____

   _____

4. dark _____

   _____

5. near _____

   _____

6. weekly _____

   _____

7. after _____

   _____

DIRECTIONS   **Secondary word classes** are subdivisions of a part of speech (such as count and noncount nouns or transitive and intransitive verbs). Write sentences using the words in the secondary word classes specified.

8. glass noncount _____

   count _____

9. run intransitive _____

   transitive _____

10. talk intransitive _____

   complex-transitive _____

11. Spanish nongradable _____

   gradable _____

App I.4   Sound Change and Word Formation   (Ref: CGCE App I.32, 43)

DIRECTIONS   When a word shifts its part of speech, there may be a change in its pronunciation. What pronunciation change marks each of these sets?

1. verb: conduct, compress, convict, ferment, subject, permit

   noun: conduct, compress, convict, ferment, subject, permit

   _____

2. adjective: frequent, absent, present, perfect

   verb: frequent, absent, present, perfect

   _____

3. noun: proof, wreath, device

   verb: prove, wreathe, devise

   _____

DIRECTIONS   There are several kinds of **reduplicative compounds.** How do the groups of compounds differ?

4. ack-ack, buddy-buddy, hush-hush, putt-putt, so-so

   _____

5. hum-drum, hob-nob, nitty-gritty, pow-wow, willy-nilly

   _____

6. chit-chat, flim-flam, ping-pong, tick-tock, wig-wag

   _____

DIRECTIONS   What minor principles of word formation are illustrated by the following groups of slang words? Use what you know about English to answer.

7. ofay, amskray, uzzfay, ixnay

   _____

8. vroom, ding-a-ling, wham-bam, yackety-yack

   _____

9. anyhoo, cowcumber, kee-rect, martooni, strumberry

   _____

App I.5 Compounding (Ref: CGCE App I.33–42)

DIRECTIONS Many **compounds** can be paraphrased roughly as phrases or clauses. Match each group of compounds below with one of the following types of paraphrase by writing the letter of the group in the blank.

1. A *blackboard* is a board that is black. _____

2. A *plaything* is a thing with which you play. _____

3. A *windmill* is a mill that is operated by wind. _____

4. *Insect repellent* is something that repels insects. _____

5. A *bartender* is one that tends bar. _____

6. A *cold wave* is a wave of cold. _____

7. A *cutthroat* is one that cuts throats. _____

8. A *sunburn* is the result of the sun burning. _____

9. A *redskin* is one that has (a) red skin. _____

10. *Candlelight* is light made by a candle. _____

11. A *piggybank* is a bank that looks like a piggy. _____

12. A *crybaby* is a baby that cries. _____

13. A *pull-toy* is a toy that one pulls. _____

14. *Birth control* is the result of controlling birth. _____

a. fry pan, washcloth, swimsuit, order blank, passkey, scrub board

b. dodge ball, drawstring, flash card, push button, throw rug

c. do-nothing, killjoy, pickpocket, sawbones, scarecrow, skinflint, daredevil

d. eyestrain, bloodshed, watch repair, book review, blood test, tax cut

e. tax collector, eye opener, lifesaver, lie detector, mind reader

f. rock candy, catfish, dragonfly, frogman, finger sandwich

g. fireball, raindrop, snowflake, cornmeal, snowman, chocolate bar

h. darkroom, gentleman, highchair, hothouse, madman, goldfish

i. flyboy, glowworm, hangman, playboy, popcorn, slide rule, sneak thief

j. blueblood, dimwit, hardtop, highbrow, loudmouth, paleface, tenderfoot

k. snakebite, earthquake, daybreak, cloudburst, landslide, plane crash

l. water wheel, steamroller, paddle boat, coal furnace, cable car, air rifle

m. noise filter, blood donor, freight elevator, coffee mill, rat trap

n. fingerprint, growing pains, hay fever, inkblot, moth hole, soapsuds

App I.6   Clipping, Blending, Acronymy   (Ref: CGCE 1.44–46; WNCD)

DIRECTIONS   What is the full form of each of these **clipped forms?**

1. mike _____
2. lab _____
3. gym _____
4. ad _____
5. bike _____
6. memo _____
7. auto _____
8. zoo _____
9. intercom _____
10. dorm _____
11. plane (airship) _____
12. bus _____
13. gator _____
14. croc _____
15. possum _____
16. mum _____

DIRECTIONS   From what pair of words was each of the following **blends** formed?

17. Amerindian _____
18. guesstimate _____
19. cafetorium _____
20. motel _____
21. medicare _____
22. smog _____
23. quasar _____
24. brunch _____
25. slurbs _____
26. motorcade _____

DIRECTIONS   From what expression was each of the following **acronyms** formed?

27. UFO _____
28. TV _____
29. KO _____
30. MC _____
31. GNP _____
32. ESP _____
33. ZIP _____
34. AWOL _____
35. SCUBA _____
36. RADAR _____

App II.1   Stress in Words and Phrases   (Ref: CGCE App II.1–4)

DIRECTIONS   Indicate the position of the **main stress** in each word by writing a raised vertical stroke before the stressed syllable.

EXAMPLES   ˈtel e graph   teˈleg ra phy   tel eˈgraph ic

1. pass ive	8. be nev o lent ly	15. per mit (*n.*)
2. re sult	9. spec u la tive ly	16. sus pect (*v.*)
3. av er age	10. Man i to ba	17. sus pect (*n.*)
4. to bac co	11. Min ne ap o lis	18. fre quent (*v.*)
5. de com pose	12. con test (*v.*)	19. fre quent (*a.*)
6. ul ti mate ly	13. con test (*n.*)	20. min ute (*n.*)
7. par tic u lar	14. per mit (*v.*)	21. mi nute (*a.*)

DIRECTIONS   Indicate the positions of the stresses in each expression by writing a raised vertical stroke for the **main stress** and a lowered vertical stroke for **secondary stress.** Write the strokes before the stressed syllables.

EXAMPLES   ˈearthˌquake   ˌfirstˈrate

1. shoe string	5. vice president	9. fire proof
2. tight rope	6. bay window	10. knee deep
3. wise crack	7. home rule	11. sour milk
4. after thought	8. after noon	12. sour puss

13. cross word (angry word)	19. white cap (cap that's white)
14. cross word (puzzle)	20. white cap (ocean foam)
15. dark room (room that's dark)	21. blue print (print that's blue)
16. dark room (photographic room)	22. blue print (house plan)
17. heavy weight (big load)	23. sleeping partner (secret partner)
18. heavy weight (boxer)	24. sleeping partner (bedmate)

App II.2   Contrastive Stress; Rhythm

(Ref: CGCE App II.5–6)

DIRECTIONS   Indicate the position of **contrastive stress** by writing a double vertical stroke before the syllables with contrastive stress.

EXAMPLE   (—John and Mary went.)—John "and Mary?

1. I said his explanation was allusive, not elusive.
2. Are you related to the John Paul Jones?
3. Thomas Sheridan wrote the dictionary, rather than Richard Sheridan.
4. I know he's not here now, but was he?
5. Though we asked him to be patient, he was impatient.

DIRECTIONS   Write a double stroke before the syllable with the strongest stress in the sentence, the **nucleus.**

EXAMPLE   She is looking "happy tonight.

6. He finished his term paper yesterday.
7. Yesterday he finished writing his paper.
8. She told her roommate about it.
9. She told her roommate about everything.
10. I think the doorbell's ringing.

DIRECTIONS   Indicate the **rhythm** of the following sentences by writing single strokes before the stressed syllables and a double stroke before the syllable with the strongest stress in the sentence.

EXAMPLE   ,She was 'looking "happy to'night.

11. The bus driver shut the door and drove off.
12. She put her package on the counter and left it there.
13. That's the gallery he sold his painting to.
14. Who told you that poker is a game of skill?
15. Why is Herman standing in the gold fish pond?

App II.3   Intonation

(Ref: CGCE App II.7–10)

DIRECTIONS   Indicate the **falling tone** by writing a grave mark (`) over the **nucleus** of each **tone unit**. A vertical bar indicates the end of each tone unit.

EXAMPLE   That's the address he sent the lètter to.|

1. Alice was reading a magazine.|
2. Who dropped this banana peel?|
3. The audience gave the performer a big hand clap.|
4. They gave him a hand clap,| not a hand clasp.|
5. Who is it,| and what does he want?|

DIRECTIONS   Indicate the **rising tone** by an acute mark (´) and the falling tone by a grave mark (`) over the nucleus of the tone unit.

EXAMPLE   I saw him this mórning,| and invited him to dìnner.|

6. Did you watch the races?|
7. One,| two,| three,| four,| and five.|
8. Because they ran out of coffee,| we had tea.|
9. They gave a party,| and invited their neighbors.|
10. It's five o'clock already?|

DIRECTIONS   Indicate the tone in each tone unit that has none marked. The tones to be added are specified for each group of sentences.

Fall-Rise (ˇ)   1. He'll do it if you ask him.|

2. Confidentially,| they're moving to Detròit.|

Rise-Fall (ˆ)   3. What a lucky thing!|

4. But that's dreadful!|

Level (ˉ)   5. It was late;| she was tired;| so she lèft.|

6. You do that,| and you'll be sòrry.|

App II.4 Prosody and Punctuation (Ref: CGCE App II.11, App III)

DIRECTIONS   Indicate the tones and tone units.

EXAMPLE   Fĭnally,| we decided not to gò.|

1. She doesn't talk to just anyone.
2. She never talks to anyone.
3. Who's driving the car?   (simple request for information)
4. Who's driving the car!?   (I can hardly believe what you said.)
5. If the band plays,   we can dance.
6. The light turns red,   traffic stops.
7. Ambrosia is made from oranges,   bananas,   pineapple,   and coconut.

DIRECTIONS   Add **punctuation marks** where they are needed.

EXAMPLE   When she saw him⸔ she laughed⸻I don't know why⊙

8. You can use a ballpoint a felt tip or even an old fashioned fountain pen whichever you like
9. They sang Korean folksongs and then the girls did a drum dance
10. Wherever they hid the book its well hidden
11. Excuse me but can you tell me how to get to town officer
12. Sam Jones who was the mayor last year has moved and plans to run for governor now
13. The capital of Puerto Rico San Juan is the largest city on the island
14. Meteorologists or so Ive heard can predict the weather with great accuracy
15. The time has come the Walrus said to speak of many things
16. The children ate a lot of schleck as grandmother used to call it

BENJAMIN BANNEKER

Pioneering Scientist

BY GINGER WADSWORTH
ILLUSTRATIONS BY CRAIG ORBACK

On My Own
BIOGRAPHY

Carolrhoda Books, Inc./Minneapolis

The illustrator would like to thank the models who were used for the oil paintings, especially J,Khaylaughn Lewis, Thaddeus Turner, and Fredrick Brown, who represent the various ages of Benjamin, as well as Gary and Eileen Orback and the Lewis family, who represent assorted characters. Thanks also to Jessica Silks for her help with photography.

The photographs on page 46 appear courtesy of © U.S. Postal Service (top) and © Bettmann/CORBIS (bottom).

This book is available in two editions:
Library binding by Carolrhoda Books, Inc., a division of Lerner Publishing Group
Soft cover by First Avenue Editions, an imprint of Lerner Publishing Group
241 First Avenue North
Minneapolis, MN 55401 U.S.A.

Website address: www.lernerbooks.com

Library of Congress Cataloging-in-Publication Data

Wadsworth, Ginger.
    Benjamin Banneker / by Ginger Wadsworth ; illustrations by Craig Orback.
      p.   cm. — (On my own biography)
    Summary: Introduces Benjamin Banneker, a free black man of the eighteenth century who loved to learn and used his knowledge and observations to build a wooden clock, write an almanac, and help survey the streets of Washington, D.C.
      ISBN: 0–87614–916–6 (lib. bdg. : alk. paper)
      ISBN: 0–87614–104–1 (pbk. : alk. paper)
    1. Banneker, Benjamin, 1731–1806—Juvenile literature. 2. Astronomers—United States—Biography—Juvenile literature. 3. African American scientists—Biography—Juvenile literature. [1. Banneker, Benjamin, 1731–1806. 2. Astronomers. 3. African Americans—Biography.] I. Orback, Craig, ill. II. Title. III. Series.
    QB36.B22 W34 2003
    520'.92—dc21   2002000985

Manufactured in the United States of America
1 2 3 4 5 6 – SP – 08 07 06 05 04 03

In memory of William "Unk" Brobeck,
Pioneer Inventor and Engineer —G.W.

For Michael O'Dwyer in New Zealand,
another inquisitive mind —C.S.O.

Maryland

1737

Benjamin Banneker was working
on his family's tobacco farm.
It was hard work for a six-year-old boy.
The sun baked his back
as he cut weeds with his hoe.
He picked bugs off the big, flat leaves.
Sometimes he counted the bugs,
just before he squished them.

He counted all the rows of tobacco
plants on the farm.
He even counted logs in the cabin he shared
with his parents and three sisters.
Counting made the lonely work
a little more fun.

At supper, Benjamin listened to stories
about his family.

Benjamin's grandmother was white.

She had been a servant long ago.

She worked for many years without pay.

Benjamin's grandfather was black.

In Africa, he had been the son of a king.

In America, he had been a slave.

Benjamin's father had been a slave, too.

But no one in Benjamin's family
was a slave anymore.

Their owners had set them free.

Now the Bannekers owned this farm.

Benjamin and his family were lucky.

Most black men, women, and children
in America were slaves.

They did not own anything.

After supper, Benjamin sat

with Grandmother Molly in her cabin.

A fire heated the little house.

Candles lit the room.

Grandmother Molly opened her Bible.

It was the only book she owned.

Grandmother was teaching Benjamin to read.

Benjamin was a fast learner.

Everyone in the family was proud of him.

He could read and write.

And he was especially good

at doing math problems.

After Grandmother Molly had taught

Benjamin everything she could,

she sent him to school.

Benjamin had never seen so many books!

Most of the students at school had white skin,

like Grandmother Molly.

Everyone sat on benches

and listened to the teacher.

Sometimes they did math problems.

Other times, they read from books.

The teacher even let Benjamin take

some books home.

Benjamin worked hard and learned a lot.

After school, he did chores.

Then, if he was not too sleepy,

he could read his school books.

At night, Benjamin lay on his bed
and looked out the window.
Stars sparkled in the inky-black sky.
Some were brighter than others,
and Benjamin wondered why.
Some groups of stars looked like
animals or shapes.
Sometimes a star seemed to shoot
across the sky.
Benjamin wondered why.

The Clock Maker

After only four years of school,
Benjamin had to quit.
He was young and strong.
His family needed him
to work on the farm full time.

But school had made Benjamin
hungry to learn.
He still kept his eyes on the sky.
Sometimes he did hard
math problems in the dirt.
He used a stick instead of a pencil.
At night, Benjamin read books by candlelight.

Like most farmers,

Benjamin told time by watching

the position of the sun.

But sometimes the sun was hidden

behind trees or clouds.

Clocks had been around for a long time.

But in the 1750s,

only rich people had clocks.

Benjamin decided to make his own.

When he was 20 years old,

Benjamin borrowed a friend's pocket watch.

He took it apart and studied each tiny piece.

How did the thin hands go around

and around, ticking off each minute?

He drew a sketch of each piece.

Then he carved new parts out of wood.

He worked on his clock

through the winter and summer.

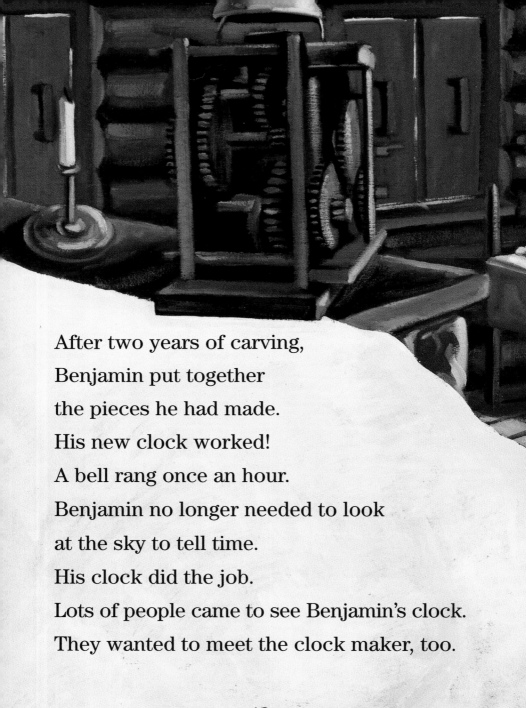

After two years of carving,
Benjamin put together
the pieces he had made.
His new clock worked!
A bell rang once an hour.
Benjamin no longer needed to look
at the sky to tell time.
His clock did the job.
Lots of people came to see Benjamin's clock.
They wanted to meet the clock maker, too.

When Benjamin was 27 years old,

the lonely farm life got even lonelier.

His father died.

His sisters had married and moved away.

And Grandmother Molly had died.

Only Benjamin and his mother were left

to do all the farm work.

There was so much to do,

Benjamin had little time for studying.

Sometimes he stayed up late

and read his math books.

Some nights he played his flute or violin

and thought about his father.

Benjamin began to make friends with
other farmers who lived nearby.
Many could not read or write.
They didn't know much about math, either.
Benjamin showed his new friends
how to weigh their tobacco crop.
He helped them figure out
how much it was worth.
He also helped them write letters.
Benjamin often met other farmers
at a nearby store.
They read newspapers there and talked
about the tough questions of farming.
Was it time to plow?
Was it going to snow again?
Was it too early to plant seeds?
Maybe someday Benjamin could help
his friends with these questions, too.

Revolution!
1775

After Benjamin's mother died,
he had to run the whole farm by himself.
It was harder than ever to find time to study.
At least he had friends at the store
to keep him company.

Important news gave Benjamin
and his friends a lot to talk about.
Maryland was one of 13 American
colonies ruled by Great Britain.
Many Americans thought the colonies
should be free to rule themselves.
They did not like paying taxes
to the British king.

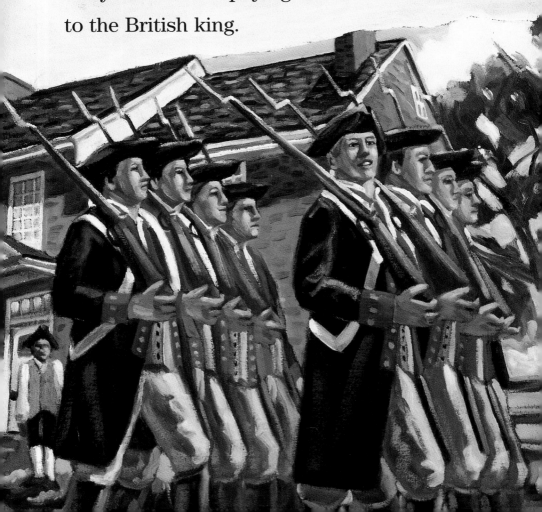

In April, British soldiers attacked
Americans in Massachusetts.
The Americans quickly formed an army.
George Washington was their leader.
Soldiers marched up and down the roads
near Benjamin's farm.
A war had begun.

After many battles, the colonies won
the Revolutionary War in 1783.
A new country was born!
George Washington became the first
president of the United States of America.

During the war, Benjamin had
kept farming and studying.
He had also begun learning a new skill.
His friend, George Ellicott, was a surveyor.
George measured land and made plans
so new roads could be built.
He taught Benjamin about surveying.
As usual, Benjamin wanted to learn
more and more.

29

George also taught Benjamin
about astronomy.
Astronomy is the science of studying
the Sun, Moon, stars, and planets.
George even had a telescope.
Benjamin had always wondered
about the stars.

Now he learned that the brightest stars
were not stars at all.
They were distant planets.
Benjamin studied George's astronomy books.
He learned how to follow the positions
of the planets.
With this information, Benjamin could tell
what the weather would be like next year.
His new knowledge also made him
a better surveyor.

There was so much to learn!
Sometimes Benjamin stayed up
studying all night.
He thought about his farmer friends.
Benjamin thought he could help them
with their farming questions.
He wanted to write an almanac.
In the 1700s, almanacs were
important books.
New ones came out every year.
They gave people information
for every day in the year.
Almanacs had calendars
and dates for planting and harvesting.
They also told what the weather
would be like the next year.
Some almanacs had poems, stories,
recipes, and news.

Benjamin dipped his pen in the ink bottle
over and over again.

Piles of paper covered his table.

On some, he had written math problems.

Some had notes about the sky
and the weather.

When the rooster crowed,

Benjamin put away his work.

It was time to milk the cows.

In 1790, President Washington chose a site
to build America's capital city.
The area was called the District of Columbia.
It was only a few hours away
from Benjamin's farm.
The president needed surveyors
to plan the streets.
The top surveyor on the job was
Andrew Ellicott, George's cousin.
Andrew knew that Benjamin was very good
at surveying and astronomy.
He asked Benjamin to help him.

Helping to survey the capital was
a great honor for Benjamin.
Very few black people in the 1790s got
a chance to do such important work.
And it was fun, too.
Benjamin loved using Andrew's excellent
surveying tools.
Benjamin worked during the cold, damp,
winter nights.
Sometimes he slept only
a few hours in his tent.
After three months, the work and weather
were wearing Benjamin down.
He was almost 60 years old.
He loved his job,
but he was ready to go home.
It was time to finish his almanac.

Almanac Writer

1791

At home, Benjamin wrote and wrote.

When he stopped, it was only to sharpen

his pen tip with his knife.

He checked his math many times.

Sometimes he forgot to do the farm chores.

It took Benjamin four months

to write an almanac for the year 1792.

His book was packed with information

that people needed—especially farmers.

Benjamin made four copies of his almanac
in his best penmanship.
He sent one copy to Thomas Jefferson.
Jefferson was the secretary of state
of the United States.
He was also a farmer, like Benjamin.
Like many white farmers,
Jefferson owned slaves.

Benjamin sent a long letter to Jefferson
along with the almanac.
He wrote that slavery was cruel.
Black people deserved to be treated
the same as white people.
He argued that no one should own slaves—
not even important American leaders.
A few weeks later, Benjamin received
a letter from Jefferson.
Jefferson thanked Benjamin
for his almanac.
He said he hoped things
would improve in the future
for black people.
But Jefferson did not free his slaves.

A book publisher wanted to print
and sell Benjamin's almanac.
It was the first published almanac
written by a black person.
Printed on the cover were the words
Benjamin Banneker's Almanac.
The publisher sold many copies,
and Benjamin became famous.
People wrote him letters,
thanking him for the helpful information.
They came to his cabin to meet him,
just as they had when he built the clock.
Benjamin stayed busy.
He had to write an almanac for 1793.
And he wrote one for the next year, too.
He wrote a new almanac every year
for six years.

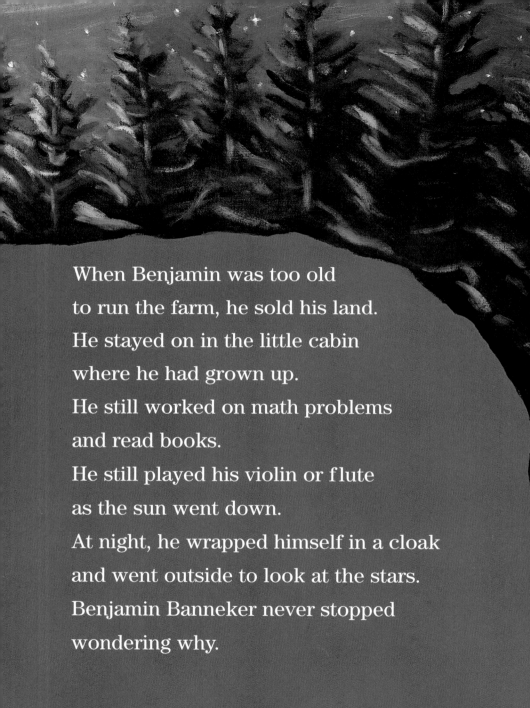

When Benjamin was too old
to run the farm, he sold his land.
He stayed on in the little cabin
where he had grown up.
He still worked on math problems
and read books.
He still played his violin or flute
as the sun went down.
At night, he wrapped himself in a cloak
and went outside to look at the stars.
Benjamin Banneker never stopped
wondering why.

In 1980, the United States Post Office issued a Benjamin Banneker stamp.

Benjamin Bannaker's PENNSYLVANIA, DELAWARE, MARYLAND, AND VIRGINIA ALMANAC, FOR THE YEAR of our LORD 1795; Being the Third after Leap-Year.

BANNAKER.

PHILADELPHIA:
Printed for WILLIAM GIBBONS, Cherry Street

The title page from one of Benjamin's almanacs. He spelled his name *Bannaker,* but it was later changed to *Banneker.*

Afterword

Benjamin Banneker died in 1806 at the age of 75. The day he was buried, his log cabin burned to the ground. Almost everything Benjamin owned was lost, including his wooden clock and his books. His sisters saved Grandmother Molly's Bible.

Benjamin and his family lived in freedom during a time when most black people in the American colonies were slaves. Many white people believed that black people were stupid and were only fit to be slaves. Some whites even tried to capture free black people and force them into slavery. Because Benjamin did not have any papers saying he was legally free, he had to worry about being made a slave.

Most black people never got a chance to prove that they were equal. But Benjamin did. People noticed what he accomplished. His almanacs and his surveying work helped prove that a person's abilities are not connected to skin color. Benjamin Banneker is remembered as a brilliant thinker and our country's first black man of science.

Important Dates

1731—Benjamin Banneker is born on November 9 in the British colony of Maryland.

1750s—Builds a wooden clock using the pieces of a pocket watch as a model

1759—Father dies

about 1775—Mother dies (the exact date of her death is not known)

1783—The United States wins its freedom when the Revolutionary War ends.

1789—George Washington becomes the first president of the United States.

1791—Benjamin helps survey the District of Columbia, where America's capital city will be.

1792—First almanac is published; sends one copy to Thomas Jefferson and makes argument against slavery

1797—Last almanac is published

1806—Dies at his cabin in Maryland